Shakespeare in the Classroom

Plays for the Intermediate Grades

Dr. Albert Cullum

FEARON TEACHER AIDS

Editorial Director: Virginia L. Murphy
Editor: Carolea Williams
Copyeditor: Susan Eddy
Cover Design: Lucyna Green
Cover and Inside Illustration: Helen Kunze
Inside Design: Diann Abbott

Fearon Teacher Aids
A Division of Frank Schaffer Publications, Inc.
23740 Hawthorne Boulevard,
Torrance, CA 90505-5927

ISBN 0–86653–903–4

Printed in the United States of America
1. 9 8 7 6 5 4 3

Contents

Introduction

For the past twenty years, Shakespeare has been one of my basic sources for teaching language arts to young students. To retell a Shakespearean story and hear a hush engulf your classroom or to invite students to roll upon their tongues poetic couplets that have enchanted listeners for years are just some of the rewarding joys of experiencing Shakespeare with children.

Shakespeare has lived through the centuries not only because of his lyrical poetry and his exciting narratives, but also because he clearly defines the good and evil of his characters and situations. Shakespeare never clouds his viewpoints nor obscures his opinions. Right is always triumphant and evil is always destroyed.

All that children need to enjoy reading or acting Shakespeare is to see and feel a teacher's love and enthusiasm for him. Hundreds of my students through the years have experienced Shakespeare as part of their world. When students make friends with William Shakespeare, they remain friends for a lifetime.

Self-Discovery

Students who are given opportunities to participate in classroom theater will gain a greater understanding of themselves and others. Through drama, students can place themselves in an imaginary world. In this world, students can identify with heroic deeds and silly laughter. Students can begin to express opinions without having to prove what they feel. Drama in the classroom is not intended to prepare children for professional acting careers but simply to give them an opportunity to express and experience genuine human emotions.

Every child in your class will find a place in the play. Some will want major roles, other smaller parts, and some will want to work backstage. A week after the first rehearsal, everyone will want to participate. That's the whole purpose of reading and producing Shakespeare—to involve children with great words, great thoughts, and moods that will inspire them to self-discovery.

Hughes Mearns in his book *Creative Power* (Dover, 1959) states the case for classroom dramatics persuasively:

> "A higher appreciation of art always follows dramatization whether it be of literature or history or geography. A child who feels the wind in his limbs, soars as a bird, and whose body opens as a bursting flower experiences these events with a deeper meaning. And those children who danced and sang in the imaginary valley all their days will feel the nearness of those mountains which have once been themselves, and they will be better for it!"

Literature Appreciation

Classroom drama can serve as an excellent introduction to great literature. Two of the reasons classical literature has lasted for centuries are that it deals with universal human themes and it can be interpreted on many intellectual and emotional levels. As educators, we are sometimes overly concerned that young children will not understand literary characters and situations. Unfortunately, this attitude too often reflects our own shortcomings and uncertainties about the classics. Don't worry if students do not comprehend all the subtleties and psychological implications of the plays. They will grasp the dominant ideas and understand the motivations at their own levels, and they will astound you with their perceptiveness. The plays have been adapted for young readers with care being taken to preserve the beauty, the power, and the humanity of the originals.

Curriculum Integration

Classical dramatic literature also supports many areas of the curriculum. Use the plays as a means of extending vocabulary. In the Shakespearean plays presented in this resource, words are often repeated from play to play. Students will have opportunities for "instant review" or "instant replay" as they meet the same words in a variety of situations. Developing vocabulary in this manner is a meaningful learning experience. After reading and discussing the plays, students could easily add several hundred words to their vocabulary.

Reading a Shakespearean play can be a delightful change of pace. Classical literature brings out many parallels with contemporary problems. After reading one of the plays together as a class, invite students to share and discuss their opinions. If given the opportunity, students will amaze you with their depth of understanding.

Creating Positive Experiences

- Don't teach Shakespeare . . . share it! For example, when introducing Hamlet, whisper these lines over and over to establish an air of mystery.

  "The play's the thing
  Wherein I'll catch the conscience of the king!"

  Students will be intrigued by the couplet. Questions about what a conscience is and how it is possible to capture it become lively discussion starters. Remember that students are beginners in the world of Shakespeare. Their appreciation of the poetic language will grow over time.

- Outline the story sequence when beginning a new play. Once the outline of the story is understood, there are a myriad of techniques that can be used to encourage further involvement. Ask students to communicate their reactions and opinions to the story.

- Without being too analytical, help students gain a better appreciation for new words they will encounter. For example, after reading Romeo and Juliet, continue to focus on the magic of Shakespeare's poetry and words by reciting:

  Benvolio: The Prince will doom thee to death if thou are caught. Run! Run!
  Romeo: I am fortune's fool!
  Benvolio: Why dost thou stay! Run!
  Prince: Where are the vile beginners of this ________?

  Encourage the listeners to step into the unknown world of Shakespeare and attempt to guess the missing word. Very few children will even come close to guessing "fray" because it is not an everyday word. But with hints and context clues, children will soon discover the meaning of the word *fray* and add it to their vocabulary.

- After you have read the play aloud once for the class, ask for volunteers to read various roles. Give every student an opportunity to read any part in which interest is shown. You will discover that almost every child will want to read a part. Even those who don't volunteer to read out loud will listen and become involved. Through these relaxed readings you will arrive at a fairly good idea of how to cast the play. Don't hesitate to double cast the main roles. Remember that boys can play girl's parts and vice versa.

- When the children feel comfortable with a play and happy with the roles they will portray, it is the time to enter the magical atmosphere of the theater. Rather than have the children stay backstage while waiting their turns to perform, suggest they scatter about the auditorium in various seats so they can see what is going on.
- Start slowly. At your first auditorium rehearsal, attempt only two or three scenes. Don't bother about interpretation or stage movement, but simply let the children get the feel of reading a script from a stage. Relax! Don't impose adult standards upon your cast. That does not mean to lower the standards but simply to respect the directness of each young actor.
- Approximately half an hour a day for about two weeks is all the time needed to prepare a successful play. Feel free to make revisions in the scripts to suit your particular class or grade level.
- Invite children to choreograph their own movement. Encourage children to use any kind of arm and hand gestures or none at all. Respect student input and ideas. Presenting plays in the classroom can be a highly creative experience if the approach is child-oriented. Don't concentrate on the final product as much as the process of getting there.
- Don't use prompters. Tell the students to ad lib if they forget their lines. Children usually don't and won't forget lines if they see that their classroom director is relaxed.
- Keep it simple. The simpler the production, the more effective it is! As the director, your concern should not be scenery, costumes, staging, or lighting, but simply one thing—to demonstrate to your students your love for Shakespeare.
- Provide encouragement. Not only do you have the privilege of introducing great literature to young, imaginative minds, but you have the priceless opportunity of giving children the gift of believing in themselves.

Hamlet

Introduction

Hamlet is a play that is synonymous with the words *intrigue* and *mystery.* One reason Hamlet is such a universally popular play is that it can be interpreted on many levels. The main theme is the revenge burning in Hamlet's heart and his efforts to discover and prove that his uncle (stepfather) is the murderer of his real father.

The moods and actions of the story move at a rapid pace. From the moment the ghost appears to the final fencing match between Hamlet and Laertes, there is a fast movement of characters on and off the stage.

Staging

Scene 1
The first scene takes place on a platform wall of Elsinore Castle. It can be staged in front of the curtain in a darkened auditorium. The actors can point to the rear of the auditorium to indicate the arrival of the ghost. The ghost should never actually appear but be left to the imagination.

Scenes 2-3
The curtain opens to reveal the throne room in the castle. Two large chairs can serve as thrones for the King and Queen. Place the chairs on a raised platform to create a more majestic look.

Scene 4
The scene again returns to a platform wall of the castle staged in front of the curtain.

Scene 5
The curtain opens as Hamlet follows the ghost of his father onto the bare stage. (The thrones and platform have been removed during Scene 4.)

Scenes 6-7
These two scenes take place in front of the curtain.

Scene 8
During scenes 6 and 7, rebuild the throne room (behind the curtain) with a raised platform and chairs. The curtain opens for Scene 8.

Scene 9
This scene, a room in the castle, can be staged in front of the curtain.

Scene 10
Curtain opens to the Queen's room with just one chair and a large piece of cloth hanging behind it to hide Polonius.

Scene 11
The scene in the castle hall can be performed in front of the curtain.

Scene 12
Curtain opens on throne room where thrones and platform are in place for the final and most memorable scene.

Costumes

Costumes are simple to prepare. Boys can wear tights or tightly fitting trousers and use corduroy or velvet skirts as capes. Girls can wear old evening gowns with pointed paper caps with a piece of chiffon attached to the tip. Children can make their own wooden swords.

Vocabulary

Scene 1
blast
consent
eruption
fantasy
harrows
illusion
nay
offended
opinion
scholar
stalks
stirring
unfold

Scene 2
apparition
assumes
beseech
cast
commendable
coronation
deeds
fie
foul
frailty
gape
grief
immediate
intent

kin	particular	'twixt
mock	preserve	unmanly
mourning	reply	warrant
overwhelm	thrice	
Scene 3	censure	tenders
embark	judgement	affection
permanent	humbly	vows
effect		
Scene 4	deprive	petty
artery	goblin	shrewdly
beckon	kettle drum	summit
bray		
Scene 5	methinks	tormenting
commandment	orchard	trivial
cursed	pursuest	villain
custom	secure	wither
joint		
Scene 6	repel	violence
desperate		
Scene 7	glean	quarters
afflicts	humbly	raves
arras	indifferent	remedy
brevity	insert	remorseless
conscience	justly	rogue
contrive	lobby	tedious
deceived	mirth	thence
declension	observe	tokens
define	peasant	transformation
delight	presence	treacherous
encounter	promontory	urged
entitled	provoke	wit
entreat		
fishmonger		
Scene 8	conduct	heir
aloof	crafty	judgements
amazement	distracted	lisp
amble	fevered	lunacy
anon	fortune	narrator
circumstances	frankly	neglected

nephew	overthrown	probe
nunnery	perchance	restore
outrageous		
Scene 9	intention	rank
horrid	rage	wretched
Scene 10	foe	remembrance
avoid	foils	repent
battalions	intruding	reputation
blush	mission	rosemary
budge	motive	shreds
cleft	nonny	thrust
columbines	pitiful	tread
condone	pranks	turf
dotes	prefer	twain
envious	quality	withered
esteem	rash	wringing
Scene 11	exceed	wager
acquainted		
Scene 12	incensed	slain
dally	justly	thine
embrace	potion	treachery
exchange	proclaim	villainy
flights		

Characters

Claudius, King of Denmark and Hamlet's stepfather
Gertrude, Queen of Denmark and Hamlet's mother
Hamlet, Prince of Denmark
Polonius, Lord Chamberlain
Horatio, Hamlet's best friend
Laertes, Polonius' son
Ophelia, Polonius' daughter
Rosencrantz, courtier
Guildenstern, courtier
Osric, courtier
Marcellus, officer
Bernardo, officer
Francisco, officer
Ghost, Hamlet's father
Players
Ladies in Waiting
Lords and Ladies of the Court

Hamlet

Scene 1: A Platform on the Wall of Elsinore Castle
(Francisco is pacing the platform.)

Bernardo: (Entering.)
Halt! Who goes there?

Francisco: Nay. Answer me. Stand and unfold yourself!

Bernardo: Long live the king!

Francisco: Bernardo?

Bernardo: Yes.

Francisco: You come most carefully upon your hour.

Bernardo: 'Tis now struck twelve. Get thee to bed, Francisco.

Francisco: For this relief, much thanks, 'tis bitter cold.

Bernardo: Have you had a quiet guard?

Francisco: Not a mouse stirring.

Bernardo: Well, good night. If you do meet Horatio and Marcellus, bid them make haste.

Francisco: I think I hear them.

Marcellus: (Entering.)
Hello! Bernardo!

Bernardo: What, is Horatio there?

Horatio: (Entering.)
Yes.

Bernardo: Welcome, Horatio. Welcome, good Marcellus.

Marcellus: What! Has this thing appeared again tonight?

Bernardo: I have seen nothing.

Marcellus: Horatio says 'tis but our fantasy.

Horatio: Tush, tush! 'Twill not appear.

Bernardo: Sit down awhile, and let us once again tell you what we have two nights seen.

Horatio: Well, sit down, and let us hear Bernardo speak of this.

Bernardo: Last night of all, Marcellus and myself, the bell then beating one, and . . .

(Enter the ghost.)

Marcellus: Peace! Break thee off! Look, where it come again!

Bernardo: In the same figure like the king that's dead.

Marcellus: Thou art a scholar! Speak to it, Horatio.

Bernardo: Looks it not like the king? Watch it, Horatio.

Horatio: Most like the dead king! It harrows me with fear and wonder!

Bernardo: It would be spoke to.

Marcellus: Question it, Horatio.

Horatio: (Speaking to the ghost.)
What art thou? By heaven I charge thee, speak!

Marcellus: It is offended!

Bernardo: See! It stalks away!

Horatio: Stay. Speak. Speak. I charge thee, speak!

(Ghost exits.)

Marcellus: 'Tis gone and will not answer.

Bernardo: How now, Horatio. You tremble and look pale. Is not this something more than fantasy? What think you on it?

Horatio: Before my god, I might not this believe, unless I saw it with mine own eyes.

Marcellus: Is it not like the dead king?

Horatio: As thou art to thyself. Such was the very armour he wore. 'Tis strange!

Marcellus: Thus twice before hath he gone by our watch.

Horatio: I know not what it means, but in any opinion this bodes some strange eruption to our state. (Re-enter the ghost.) But soft, behold! Look! Lo, where it comes again! I'll cross it though it blast me! Stay illusion! If thou hast any voice speak to me. Stay and speak! (The cock crows.) Stop it, Marcellus!

Bernardo: 'Tis here!

Horatio: 'Tis here!

Marcellus: 'Tis gone!

(The ghost vanishes.)

Bernardo: It was about to speak when the cock crew.

Horatio: But then it vanished. But look, it's morning! Break we our watch up and by my advice, let us tell what we have seen tonight to young Hamlet. For upon my life this ghost, dumb to us, will speak to him. Do you consent we tell him?

Marcellus: Let's do it, I pray. I know where we shall find him!

Scene 2: Throne Room in the Castle That Morning

(King and Queen seated on thrones with Hamlet, Laertes, and Polonius in attendance.)

King: And now, Laertes, what's the news with you? You told us of some wish. What is it, Laertes? What wouldst thou have, Laertes?

Laertes: Your permission to return to France from where I came to Denmark to show my duty to your coronation.

King: Have you your father's permission? What says Polonius?

Polonius: He hath, my lord, my consent! I do beseech you, give him leave to go.

King: Laertes, go as you will. And now, my cousin Hamlet, and now my son—

Hamlet: (Aside.)
A little more than kin, and less than kind.

King: How is it that the clouds still hang on you?

Hamlet: Not so, my lord. I am too much in the sun.

Queen: Good Hamlet, cast thy mourning off, and let thine eye look like a friend on the King. Do not forever seek for thy noble father in the dust. Thou know'st 'tis common, all that lives must die.

Hamlet: Ay mother, it is common.

Queen: If it be, why seems it so particular with thee?

Hamlet: Seems, good mother? Nay, it is! I know not "seems."

King: 'Tis sweet and commendable in your nature Hamlet to give these mourning duties to your father. But you must know your father lost a father, that father lost his father, but to preserve this unmanly grief! Fie! 'Tis a fault to heaven, a fault against the dead. We pray you, think of us as a father, for let the world take note, you are the most immediate to our throne! For your intent in going back to school in Wittenberg, we beseech you to remain here as our son.

Queen: Let not thy mother lose her prayers, Hamlet. I pray thee, stay with us. Go not to Wittenberg.

Hamlet: I shall in all my best obey thee, mother.

King: Why 'tis a loving and a fair reply. Madam, come, come away! (Exit the King and Queen.)

Hamlet: O, that this too too solid flesh would melt. That is should come to this! My father, but two months dead, nay not so much, not even two months. So excellent a king, so loving to my mother. Heaven and earth must I remember? Why, she would hang on his every word, and yet within a month . . . let me not think of it! Frailty, thy name is woman! Within a month she married my uncle, my father's brother, but not more like my father than I to Hercules. O most wicked speed, it cannot come to good. But break my heart, for I must hold my tongue!

(Enter Horatio, Marcellus, and Bernardo.)

Horatio: Hail to your lordship!

Hamlet: I am glad to see you well, Horatio and friends. But what, in faith, is your affair in Elsinore?

Horatio: My lord, I came to see your father's funeral.

Hamlet: I pray thee, do not mock me, fellow student. I think it was to see my mother's wedding.

Horatio: My lord, I think I saw your father yesternight.

Hamlet: Saw? Who?

Horatio: My lord, the king, your father!

Hamlet: The king, my father? For God's love, let me hear!

Horatio: For two nights these gentlemen, Marcellus and Bernardo, on their watch saw a figure like your father. Thrice he walked by while they stood dumb, too afraid to speak. This they told to me, and I with them the third night kept the watch. Where, as they had said, the apparition came. I knew your father, these hands are not more like.

Hamlet: But where was this?

Marcellus: My lord, upon the platform where we watch.

Hamlet: Did you not speak to it?

Horatio: My lord, I did, but answer made it none.

Hamlet: I will watch tonight. Perhaps 'twill walk again.

Horatio: I warrant it will.

Hamlet: If it assumes my father's shape, I'll speak to it, though hell itself should gape and bid me hold my peace. I pray you all, tell no one. Fare you well. Upon the platform I'll visit you 'twixt eleven and twelve.

All: Our duty to your honor!

Hamlet: Mine to you. Farewell. (Exit all but Hamlet.) My father's spirit—all is not well. I would the night were come—'till then sit still, my soul! Foul deeds will rise through all the earth overwhelm them to men's eyes.

Scene 3: Throne Room That Afternoon

(Laertes and Ophelia are talking together.)

Laertes: I am ready to embark. And, sister, do not sleep, but let me hear from you.

Ophelia: Do you doubt that?

Laertes: Hamlet is not permanent, sweet, nor lasting. The perfume of a minute—no more!

Ophelia: No more than that?

Laertes: Think it no more. Perhaps he loves you now, but you must fear. His will is not his own, for he himself is subject to his birth. He may not, as unvalued persons do, love whom he pleases, for on his choice depends the safety and health of his whole state. Therefore if he says he loves you, fear it, Ophelia, fear it, my dear sister.

Ophelia: I shall the effect of this good lesson keep, my good brother.

Laertes: I stay too long—but here comes our father.

(Polonius enters.)

Polonius: Yet here, Laertes? Aboard, aboard, for shame! The wind sits in the shoulder of your sail, and you are stayed for. But let me give you some advice. Beware of entrance into a quarrel, but being in it, bear it, that the opposed may beware of thee. Give every man thy ear, but few thy voice. Take each man's censure, but reserve thy judgement. Neither a borrower nor a lender be, for loan often loses both itself and a friend, and borrowing dulls the edge of friendship. And most of all, to thine own self be true, and it must follow as the night the day, thou canst not then be false to any man. Farewell, my son, my blessing upon thee!

Laertes: Most humbly do I take my leave, oh father. Farewell, Ophelia, and remember well what I have said to you.

Ophelia: 'Tis in my memory locked, and you yourself shall keep the key of it.

Laertes: Farewell.

(Laertes exits.)

Polonius: What is it, Ophelia, he hath said to you?

Ophelia: So please you, something about Lord Hamlet.

Polonius: I thought so. What is it between you and Lord Hamlet? Give me the truth.

Ophelia: He hath of late, my father, made many tenders of his affection to me.

Polonius: Affection! Pooh! You speak like a child. Do you believe Lord Hamlet?

Ophelia: I do not know, my father, what I should think.

Polonius: I'll tell you. I think you a baby that you have taken these tenders of affection for true pay, which are not true sterling.

Ophelia: He hath told me of his love in honourable fashion, my father.

Polonius: Do not believe his vows. I would in plain terms from this time forth not have you speak to Lord Hamlet. Look to it, I charge you!

Ophelia: I shall obey, my father.

Scene 4: Platform on Castle Wall at Midnight
(Hamlet, Horatio, and Marcellus enter.)

Hamlet: The air bites shrewdly. It is very cold.

Horatio: It is a nipping and an eager air.

Hamlet: What hour now?

Horatio: I think it nearly twelve.

Marcellus: No, it has already struck midnight.

Horatio: Indeed? I heard it not. It then draws near the time the ghost walks. (Sound of trumpets and drums.) What does this mean, my lord?

Hamlet: The king is celebrating. The kettle drum and trumpet thus bray out his triumph.

(Enter the ghost of Hamlet's father.)

Horatio: Look, my lord, it comes!

Hamlet: Angels and ministers of grace, defend us! Be thou a spirit of health, or goblin damned, bring with thee airs from heaven or blasts from hell? Father, father . . . O answer me . . What should we do?

Horatio: It beckons you to go away with it, as if it did desire to speak to you alone.

Marcellus: Look . . . it waves to you, but do not go with it.

Horatio: No, by no means.

Hamlet: If it will not speak, then I will follow it.

Horatio: Do not, my lord.

Hamlet: Why? What should be the fear? It waves me forth again. I'll follow it!

Horatio: What if it tempt you toward the flood, my lord, or to the dreadful summit of the cliff over the sea, and there assume some other horrible form which might deprive you of reason and draw you into madness? Think of it!

Hamlet: It waves to me still! (To Ghost.) Go on, I'll follow thee.

Marcellus: You shall not go, my lord.

Hamlet: Hold off your hands!

Horatio: You shall not go!

Hamlet: My fate cries out, and makes each petty artery in this body as hardy as a lion's nerve. Unhand me! I'll make a ghost of him that holds me back. (To Ghost.) Go on, I'll follow thee!

(Exit Ghost and Hamlet.)

Horatio: Let's follow. 'Tis not fit to obey him.

Marcellus: Something is rotten in the state of Denmark.

Scene 5: Another Part of the Platform

(Hamlet and Ghost enter.)

Hamlet: Whither wilt thou lead me? Speak! I'll go no farther.

Ghost: Mark me.

Hamlet: I will.

Ghost: My hour is almost come when I to tormenting flames must render up myself.

Hamlet: Alas, poor Ghost.

Ghost: Pity me not, but lend thy serious hearing to what I shall unfold.

Hamlet: Speak! I am bound to hear.

Ghost: Thou wilt revenge when thou shalt hear.

Hamlet: What?

Ghost: I am thy father's spirit. Listen . . . listen . . . If thou didst ever thy dear father love. Revenge his foul and most unnatural murder.

Hamlet: Murder?

Ghost: Murder most foul, strange, and unnatural.

Hamlet: Hasten me to know it that I may sweep to my revenge.

Ghost: Now, Hamlet, listen! 'Tis said that sleeping in my orchard a serpent stung me. That is false! But, my noble son, the serpent that did sting thy father's life now wears his crown!

Hamlet: My uncle?

Ghost: Ay, that beast won to his side the will of my most beloved queen, your mother! O Hamlet, what a falling off was there. But soft, methinks I scent the morning air. Brief let me be. Sleeping within my orchard, my custom always of the afternoon, upon my secure hour your uncle stole close and in my ears did pour a cursed poison. O horrible! O horrible! Most horrible! Let not the throne of Denmark go unrevenged! But, however thou pursuest this act, let thy soul contrive nothing against thy mother. Leave her to heaven. Farewell. Remember me, my son. Remember thy father. Remember me!

(Exit Ghost.)

Hamlet: Remember thee? Aye, thou poor ghost! Remember thee? From my memory I'll wipe away all trivial records and thy commandment alone shall live within my brain. So uncle, there you are . . . villain. . . smiling villain! Now to my word. I have sworn it!

Horatio: What is it, my lord?

Marcellus: Lord Hamlet!

Hamlet: And now my good friends, give me one poor request.

Horatio: What is it, my lord?

Hamlet: Never make known what you have seen tonight.

Horatio and Marcellus: We will not, my lord.

Hamlet: So, gentlemen, we will leave together. And still your fingers on your lips, I pray. The time is out of joint!

Scene 6: Room in Polonius' House Two Months Later
(Polonius and Ophelia enter.)

Polonius: How now, Ophelia, what's the matter?

Ophelia: O, my father, I have been so frightened.

Polonius: With what in the name of God?

Ophelia: As I was sitting in my room, Lord Hamlet came before me with his face pale as his shirt and with a look so strange.

Polonius: Mad for thy love?

Ophelia: My father, I do not know, but truly I do fear it!

Polonius: Come with me. I will go seek the king. This is the very madness of love. His violence will lead to desperate undertakings. Have you given him any hard words of late?

Ophelia:	No, my father. I did repel his letters and denied his visits as you did command.
Polonius:	That hath made him mad. Come, we go to the king. This must be known!

Scene 7: A Room in the Castle That Afternoon
(King and Queen with Rosencrantz and Guildenstern.)

King:	Welcome, dear Rosencrantz and Guildenstern! The need we have to use you did provoke our hasty sending. I'm sure you have heard of Hamlet's transformation. What it could be other than his father's death, I cannot dream of. I entreat you both having been brought up with Hamlet, that you rest here in our castle some little time, so by your companies you may glean what afflicts him that lies within our remedy.
	(Rosencrantz and Guildenstern bow.)
Queen:	Thanks, Guildenstern and gentle Rosencrantz. And I beseech you instantly to visit my too changed son. Go, and bring these gentlemen where Hamlet is.
Guildenstern:	Heavens make our presence pleasant and helpful to him.
Queen:	Amen!
	(Exit Rosencrantz, and Guildenstern and enter Polonius and Ophelia.)
Polonius:	My good king, I do think that I have found the very cause of Hamlet's lunacy.
King:	Speak! That do I long to hear.
Polonius:	My king and queen, since brevity is the soul of wit, I will be brief. Your noble son, Lord Hamlet, is mad! Mad, call I it. For to define true madness . . .
Queen:	More matter with less art.
Polonius:	Madam, I swear I use no art at all. That he is mad 'tis true, 'tis a pity! Consider I have a daughter who in her duty hath given me this note.

Queen: Comes this from Hamlet to her?

Polonius: Yes. Good madam, patience. I will read it to you! (Polonius reads the note.) "O dear Ophelia, I am ill. I love thee best. Goodbye . . . Hamlet." I went to my daughter and told her she should lock herself in her room, admit no messengers, receive no tokens. Hamlet, repulsed, fell into a sadness, then into a fast, thence to a watch, thence into a weakness, thence to a lightness, and by this declension into the madness wherein now he raves and all we mourn for.

King: Do you think this?

Queen: It may be.

Polonius: I wish we could prove it otherwise.

King: How may we try it further?

Polonius: Sometimes he walks for hours in the lobby.

Queen: He does indeed.

Polonius: At such a time, I'll send my daughter to him. Be you and I behind an arras to mark the encounter.

King: We will try it.

Queen: But look where sadly the poor boy comes reading.

Polonius: Away, I do beseech you, both away. I'll speak to him. (Exit King, Queen and enter Hamlet.) How goes it with my good Hamlet?

Hamlet: Well.

Polonius: Do you know me, my lord?

Hamlet: Excellent well! You are a fishmonger.

Polonius: Not I, my lord.

Hamlet: Then I would you were so honest a man.

Polonius: Honest, my lord?

Hamlet: Ay sir, to be honest, as this world goes, is to be one man picked out of ten thousand.

Polonius: That's very true, my lord.

Hamlet: Have you a daughter?

Polonius: I have, my lord.

Hamlet: Look out for her, friend.

Polonius: (Aside.)
What does he mean by that? I'll speak to him again. What do you read, my lord?

Hamlet: Words, words, words!

Polonius: What is the matter, my lord?

Hamlet: Between who?

Polonius: I mean the matter that you read, my lord.

Hamlet: That you, sir, shall grow as old as I am, if like a crab you could go backward.

Polonius: (Aside.)
Though this be madness, yet there is a method in it. I will leave him and suddenly contrive the means of meeting him and my daughter. My honourable Lord Hamlet, I will most humbly take my leave of you.

Hamlet: You cannot, sir, take from me anything that I will more willingly part with except my life, except my life, except my life.

Polonius: Fare you well, my Lord Hamlet.

Hamlet: These tedious old fools!

(Enter Rosencrantz and Guildenstern.)

Polonius: You go to seek the Lord Hamlet? There he is.

Rosencrantz: God save you, sir.

(Exit Polonius.)

Guildenstern: My honoured lord.

Rosencrantz: My most dear lord.

Hamlet: My excellent good friends. Good lads, how are you both?

Rosencrantz: As the indifferent children of the earth.

Guildenstern: Happy, in that we are not overhappy.

Hamlet: But what brings you to Castle Elsinore?

Rosencrantz: To visit you, my lord, no other reason.

Hamlet: Were you not sent for? Come, deal justly with me. Come, come, speak.

Guildenstern: What should we say, my lord?

Hamlet: Why anything, but to the point! You were sent for. There is a kind of confession in your looks. I know the good king and queen have sent for you.

Rosencrantz: Why, my lord?

Hamlet: That, you must teach me. But let me beg you, be honest with me, whether you were sent for, or not. If you love me, hold not off.

Guildenstern: My lord, we were sent for.

Hamlet: I will tell you why so your word to the king and queen be not broken. I have of late, but I know not why, lost all my mirth. The earth seems to me a promontory . . . nothing delights me. Why did you smile when I said nothing delights me?

Rosencrantz: To think, my lord, what little satisfaction the players will receive from you. We urged them to come, and here they come to entertain you.

Hamlet: They are welcome, but what players are they?

Rosencrantz: Why those actors and actresses you used to take such delight in.

Guildenstern: Here are the players!

(Enter players.)

Hamlet: You are welcome to Castle Elsinore. (To Rosencrantz and Guildenstern.) But my uncle—father and mother are deceived.

Guildenstern: Deceived how, my lord?

Hamlet: I am but mad north—north west. When the wind is southerly I know a hawk from a handsaw. (To the players.) You are welcome, actors. Welcome, all! I am glad to see thee well. Welcome, good friends. (Enter Polonius.) My lord, will you see the actors to their quarters. Let them be well cared for.

Polonius: My lord, I will. Come sirs.

Hamlet: Follow him, friends. We will hear a play tomorrow. (Exit Polonius with all the actors except the first player.) Can you perform the play entitled "The Murder of Gonzago?"

First Player: Ay, my lord.

Hamlet: Good! We will have it tomorrow night. You could, if need be, study a speech of some dozen or sixteen lines which I would write and insert in the play, could you not?

First Player: Ay, my lord.

Hamlet: Very well, follow the rest. I'll leave you till night. (Exit Player. To Rosencrantz and Guildenstern.) You are welcome to Castle Elsinore.

Rosencrantz and Guildenstern: Thank you, my lord.

Hamlet: God be with you. (Rosencrantz and Guildenstern exit.) Now I am alone. O, what a rogue and peasant slave am I! Am I a coward? It cannot be that I am pigeon livered, or before now I should have revenged my father with this king—uncle's death. Remorseless, treacherous, kindless villain. What a fool am I to unpack my heart with words. But, let me think. I'll have these actors play something like the murder of my father before my uncle. I'll observe his looks. If he but turn pale, I know my course. I must have proof. The play's the thing wherein I'll catch the conscience of the king.

Scene 8: Throne Room in Castle the Next Day
(Enter King, Queen, Ophelia, Polonius, Rosencrantz, and Guildenstern.)

King: Why can't you get from him why he puts on this dangerous lunacy?

Rosencrantz: He confesses he feels himself distracted, but from what cause he will not say.

Guildenstern: But, with a crafty madness, Lord Hamlet keeps aloof when we try to talk of his odd conduct.

Queen: Did he receive you well?

Rosencrantz: Most politely.

King: Good gentlemen, try again to probe his fevered mind.

Rosencrantz: We shall, my lord!

(Exit Rosencrantz and Guildenstern.)

King: Sweet Gertrude, leave us, too. For we have sent for Hamlet that as by accident he may encounter Ophelia. Polonius and I will hide ourselves, that unseen we may judge frankly and see if it is love or not that he suffers from.

Queen: I shall obey you. And for you, Ophelia, I hope you will bring Hamlet to his senses again.

Ophelia: Madam, I wish it may be so.

(Queen exits.)

Polonius: Ophelia, stand here. We will hide ourselves. Read this book. I hear Lord Hamlet coming. Let us withdraw, my lord!

(Hamlet enters.)

Hamlet: To be, or not to be, that is the question. Whether 'tis nobler in the mind to suffer the slings and arrows of outrageous fortune, or to take arms against a sea of troubles, and by opposing, end them. To die, to sleep, and by a sleep to say we end the heartache and the thousand natural shocks that flesh is heir to. To die, to sleep, to sleep, perchance to dream. Aye, there's the rub, for in that sleep of death what dreams may come?

Ophelia: My Lord Hamlet, how are you this day?

Hamlet: I humbly thank you, well, well, well.

Ophelia: My lord, I have gifts from you that I have longed to return. I pray you now receive them.

(Ophelia attempts to return bracelets and rings.)

Hamlet: No, not I. I never gave you anything.

Ophelia: My lord, you know right well you did. Take these again, for rich gifts become poor when givers prove unkind. There, my lord. (Ophelia places jewels at his feet.)

Hamlet: Ha, ha! Are you honest?

Ophelia: My lord?

Hamlet: Are you beautiful?

Ophelia: What means your lordship?

Hamlet: I truly did love thee once!

Ophelia: You made me believe so, my lord.

Hamlet: You should not have believed me. I loved you not.

Ophelia: I was the more deceived!

Hamlet: Get thee to a nunnery. Believe none of us. Go thy ways to a nunnery. Where's your father?

Ophelia: At home, my lord.

Hamlet: Let the doors be shut upon him, that he may play the fool nowhere but in his own house. Farewell.

Ophelia: (Aside.)
O help him, you sweet heavens.

Hamlet: Get thee to a nunnery, go, farewell. Wise men know well enough what monsters you make of them. To a nunnery go, and quickly. Farewell!

Ophelia: O heavenly powers, restore him!

Hamlet: God hath given you one face, and you make yourself another. You jig, you amble, and you lisp. It hath made me mad. To a nunnery go!

(Exit Hamlet quickly and re-enter Polonius and the King from behind the drapes.)

Ophelia: O what a noble mind is here overthrown! O, woe is me, to see what I have seen.

King: Love! No it is not love that makes him mad. I fear there will be some danger. What think you of it?

Polonius: I do believe his madness springs from neglected love. Now, now, Ophelia, you need not tell us what the Lord Hamlet said, for we heard it all. My king, do as you please, but after the play let his Queen Mother talk to Hamlet alone and I'll eavesdrop. If she can't set him straight, send him to England or confine him where you think best.

King: It shall be so. Madness in great ones must not unwatched go!

(Exit King, Polonius, and Ophelia. Enter Hamlet and Horatio.)

Hamlet: The actors are ready for the play tonight before the king. One scene of it comes near the circumstances of my father's death. I pray you, when you see that scene, observe my uncle—father. If he looks not guilty, it is an evil ghost that we have seen. Watch him closely and so shall I, and after, we will compare our judgements of him.

Horatio: Very well, my lord.

Hamlet: They are coming to the play. Get you a place.

(Trumpets and drums are sounded. Enter King Claudius, Queen Gertrude, Polonius, Ophelia, Rosencrantz, Guildenstern, and lords and ladies of the court. After the King and Queen are seated, everyone else is seated, and the play begins. The play is done in pantomime. First Player is preparing to sleep in orchard.)

Hamlet: Mother, how do you like the play thus far?

Queen: Have you seen it before?

King: What do you call the play?

Hamlet: The "Mouse Trap." This play is in the image of a murder done in Vienna. Gonzago is the duke's name. His wife you shall see anon. 'Tis a knavish piece of work, but what of that? Your majesty and we that have free souls, it touches us not! (Player Two enters playing the role of Lucianus.) This is Lucianus, nephew to the king.

Ophelia: You are good as a narrator, my lord.

(Player Two begins to pour some poison into Player One's ear.)

Hamlet: He poisons the king in the garden for his estate. The king's name is Gonzago. You shall see anon how the murderer gets the love of Gonzago's wife.

(King jumps up.)

Ophelia: The king rises!

Hamlet: What? Frightened with false fire?

King: Give me some light. Away!

Hamlet: Lights! Lights! Lights!

Polonius: Stop the play!

(Exit all but Hamlet and Horatio.)

Hamlet: O good Horatio, the ghost was telling the truth. Did you see the face of the king?

Horatio: Very well, my lord.

Hamlet: Upon the talk of the poisoning?

Horatio: I did very well notice him.

Hamlet: Come! Some music, for if the king like not the play, why then give him some music!

(Re-enter Rosencrantz and Guildenstern.)

Guildenstern: My lord Hamlet, a word with you. The king, sir . . .

Hamlet: Ay, what of him?

Guildenstern: The king is very upset!

Hamlet: With drink, sir?

Guildenstern: No, my lord, he is ill.

Hamlet: Tell this to the doctor, not to me.

Guildenstern: My lord, the Queen, your mother, hath sent me to you.

Hamlet: My mother you say?

Rosencrantz: She says your behaviour struck her into amazement. She desires to speak with you in her room.

Hamlet: I shall obey were she ten times my mother!

(Re-enter Polonius.)

Polonius: My lord Hamlet, the Queen would speak with you pres ently!

Hamlet: I will come to my mother by and by. I will come by and by.

Polonius: I should hope so!

(Polonius exits.)

Hamlet: "By and by" is easily said. Leave me, friends. (Exit all but Hamlet.) Let me be firm, not cruel. I will speak daggers to her, but use none.

Scene 9: Room in the Castle a Few Minutes Later
(King is pacing up and down.)

King: O my crime is rank, it smells to heaven, a brother's murder. I cannot pray though I want to. My stronger guilt defeats my strong intention. Is there not rain enough in the heavens to wash my wrongdoing white as snow? Then I'll pray, but oh what form of prayer can I say? Forgive me my foul murder? That cannot be, for I still have those things for which I did murder, my crown, my own ambition, and my queen. O wretched state! O black soul! Help me, angels! Bow stubborn knees and heart, be soft as a newborn babe. All may be well!

(The King kneels to pray. Enter Hamlet, unnoticed by the King.)

Hamlet: Now might I do it easily, now while he is praying. And now I'll do it, and so he goes to heaven, and so am I revenged? That would be terrible! A villain kills my father and for that I send this same villain to heaven? This is not revenge. No! Up, sword, and wait for a better time. Then trip him that his heels may kick at heaven and that his soul may be damned and black as hell, whereto it goes. My mother waits for me.

(Hamlet exits.)

King: (Rising.)
My words fly up, my thoughts remain below. Words without thoughts never to heaven go.

Scene 10: Queen's Room a Little Later
(Enter Queen and Polonius.)

Polonius: He will be here soon. Look you, scold him soundly! Tell him his pranks have been too broad to condone and that you have stood between him and punishment. I'll hide behind the curtain. Pray you, be firm with him.

Queen: I will, never fear.

Hamlet: (Off stage.)
Mother! Mother! Mother!

Queen: Withdraw. He comes!

(Polonius hides behind drapes and Hamlet enters.)

Hamlet: Now, mother, what's the matter?

Queen: Hamlet, thou hast thy father much offended.

Hamlet: Mother, you have *my* father much offended.

Queen: Come, come now, you answer with a silly tongue.

Hamlet: You question with a wicked tongue.

Queen: Have you forgotten who I am?

Hamlet: Goodness no! You are the queen, your husband's brother's wife and would it were not so, you are my mother.

Queen: I'll send those to you that can deal with you.

(Queen begins to leave.)

Hamlet: Come and sit you down. You shall not budge! You leave not until I set you up a mirror where you may see the most inmost part of you.

Queen: What wilt thou do? Thou wilt not murder me? Help! Help!

Polonius: (Behind the drapery.)
Help! Help!

Hamlet: (Drawing his sword.)
How now . . . a rat? (Hamlet kills Polonius by plunging his sword through the drapes.) Dead for a penny . . . dead!

Queen: What hast thou done?

Hamlet: I know not. Is it the king?

Queen: O what a rash deed is this!

Hamlet: Almost as bad, good mother, as kill a king and marry with his brother.

Queen: As kill a king?

Hamlet: Ay mother. Those were my words. (Hamlet pulls back the drapes and sees Polonius dead.) Thou wretched, rash, intruding fool. I took thee for the king! (To Queen.) Stop wringing your hands. Sit down and let me wring your heart, for I will, if it be a human heart!

Queen: What have I done that thou darest speak so rudely to me?

Hamlet: Such an act, such a deed!

Queen: What have I done?

Hamlet: Look here upon this picture, and on this . . . the portraits of two brothers. See! This was your husband. Look you now what follows. Here is your husband! Have you eyes? Could you prefer this to this? O shame, where is thy blush?

Queen: O Hamlet, speak no more. Thou turnest mine eyes into my very soul, and there I see such black spots. O speak to me no more. These words like daggers enter in my ears. No more, sweet Hamlet!

Hamlet: He is a murderer and a villain that is not a twentieth part as good as my father. He is a thief that stole a kingdom and put it in his pocket.

Queen: No more!

Hamlet: A king of shreds and patches! (Enter Ghost.) O heavens save me. What do you desire?

Queen: Alas, he's mad!

Hamlet: Do not come to scold your son.

Ghost: Do not forget your mission. I come to remind you. But look, thy mother is afraid. Step between her and her fighting soul. Speak to her, Hamlet.

Hamlet: What is the matter, mother?

Queen: What are you looking at? Whom are you talking to?

Hamlet: On him, on him! Look how pale he is! (To the Ghost) Do not look at me with such sadness.

Queen: To whom do you speak this?

Hamlet: Do you hear nothing?

Queen: No, nothing but ourselves.

Hamlet: Why look you there! Look how it steals away! My father as he lived. Look where he goes, even now out the door!

Queen: You're mad!

Hamlet: It is not madness that I have uttered. Mother, for love of grace, don't deceive yourself. Confess to heaven, repent what's past, avoid what is to come.

Queen: O Hamlet, thou hast cleft my heart in twain.

Hamlet: O, throw away the worser part of it and live the purer with the other half. Good night, mother, and when you want to be forgiven, I'll beg of you to forgive me. (Pointing to Polonius.) For this old man I do repent. I will answer for the death I gave him. So again, good night. I must be cruel, only to be kind.

(Exit Hamlet dragging out Polonius. Enter King, Claudius, Rosencrantz, and Guildenstern.)

King: What's the matter? Tell me! Where is your son?

Queen: Ah my lord, what I have seen tonight!

King: Gertrude, how is Hamlet?

Queen: Mad as the sea and wind. He has killed good Polonius!

King: O heavy deed! It was meant for me, had I been there. His liberty is dangerous to us all, to you yourself, to every one! How shall this horrible deed be answered? Where has he gone?

Queen: To remove the body he hath killed. He weeps for what he has done.

King: Rosencrantz and Guildenstern, go get help! Hamlet in madness hath slain Polonius and from his mother's room hath dragged him. Go find him and bring the body into the chapel. I pray you, hurry! (Exit Rosencrantz and Guildenstern.) Gertrude, come away! (Exit Queen.) How dangerous it is that this Hamlet goes loose! (Enter Rosencrantz.) How now, what has happened?

Rosencrantz: Where the dead body is hidden my lord, we cannot get from him.

King: But where is Hamlet?

Rosencrantz: Outside, my lord, guarded to know your pleasure.

King: Bring him before me.

Rosencrantz: Ho, Guildenstern, bring in the Lord Hamlet.

(Enter Guildenstern with Hamlet.)

King: Now, Hamlet, where is Polonius?

Hamlet: In heaven or in the other place. But, indeed, if you find him not within the month, you will smell him as you go up the stairs into the lobby.

(Hamlet exits with Rosencrantz and Guildenstern.)

King: Somehow, I must contrive the present death of Hamlet.

(Exit King. Moments later Queen enters with her Lady in Waiting.)

Queen: I will not speak with her.

Lady in Waiting: She insists. Her mood is so pitiful.

Queen: What does she want?

Lady in Waiting: She speaks much of her father, Polonius. Her speech is senseless, yet it moves one to pity. She is very unhappy.

Queen: Let her come in. (Exit Lady in Waiting.) I too, am sick to my soul. (Enter Lady in Waiting with a mad Ophelia.)

Ophelia: Where is the beautiful Queen Gertrude?

Queen: How now, Ophelia?

Ophelia: (Singing.)
He is dead and gone, lady.
He is dead and gone,
At his head a grass green turf,
At his heels a stone.

(Enter King Claudius.)

Queen: Alas, look here, my lord.

Ophelia: (Singing.)
He is dead and gone, lady.
He is dead and gone,
At his head a grass green turf,
At his heels a stone.

King: She sings about her dead father. How long has she been thus?

Ophelia: I hope all will be well. We must be patient, but I cannot choose but weep to think they should lay him in the cold ground. My brother, Laertes, shall know of it, and so I thank you for your counsel. Good night, good night, good night, good night!

(Exit Ophelia running out madly.)

King: Follow her close. Watch her I pray you. (Exit Lady in Waiting.) Her deep grief springs from her father's death. O, Gertrude, Gertrude, when sorrows come, they come not singly, but in battalions. First her father slain, poor Ophelia near to madness, and last but not least her brother Laertes has come from France in secret, seeking the answer to his father's death.

(Much noise outside.)

Queen: Alack, what noise is this?

King: Where are my men? Let them guard the door! (Enter Second Lady in Waiting.) What is the matter?

Second Lady in Waiting: My lord, young Laertes in a riotous mood hath got past the guards. The doors are broke!

(Enter Laertes armed.)

Laertes: O, thou vile king, give me my father!

Queen: Calmly, good Laertes.

King: What is the cause of this, Laertes? Let him go, Gertrude. I am not afraid! Tell me, Laertes, why art thou thus enraged! Speak man!

Laertes: Where is my father?

King: Polonius, your father, is dead.

Queen: But not by the king.

King: Let him speak!

Laertes: How came he dead? I'll not be juggled with! Let come what comes, I'll be revenged for my father's murder!

King: Who shall stop you?

Laertes: Not all the world!

King: Good Laertes, if you desire to know the truth about your dear father's death, will you punish both friend and foe?

Laertes: None but his enemies. To his friends thus wide I'll open my arms.

King: You speak as a true gentleman. I am not guilty of your father's death.

(Noise outside.)

Laertes: How now! What noise is this? (Enter Ophelia insane.) O tears seven times salt, burn out this sight from my eyes. By heaven, thy madness shall be paid for! O dear sister, sweet Ophelia!

Ophelia: (Singing)
They bore him bare faced on the bier;
Hey non nonny, hey nonny.
And in his grave rained many a tear,
Fare you well, my dove!

Laertes: Hadst thou thy wits and did beg revenge, it could not affect me more!

Ophelia: There's rosemary, that's for remembrance. Pray you remember. There are pansies, that's for thoughts. There's roses for you and columbines. There's a daisy. I would give you some violets, but they all withered when my father died. God have mercy on his soul and all souls.

(Queen Gertrude takes Ophelia out.)

Laertes: Do you see this?

King: Laertes, you shall have satisfaction. Where the guilt is, let the axe fall. You must believe Hamlet did not intend to kill your noble father. He meant the dagger for me!

Laertes: So it would appear, but why have you let him go unpunished?

King: For two special reasons. The queen, his mother, dotes on him so and for myself, she is so necessary to my life. The other motive is the public holds Hamlet in such high esteem, that I am afraid what might happen.

Laertes: And so I have a noble father lost, and a sister driven insane. But my revenge will come.

King: True, so it shall. I loved your father, and I love my life. Can you advise me?

Laertes: Get Hamlet. I shall tell him to his teeth what he did.

King: Laertes, will you be ruled by me?

Laertes: Ay, my lord.

King: I have a plot under which Hamlet shall die, and for this death no blame shall be put on us. Even his mother shall think it an accident.

Laertes: My lord, could you arrange it so that I might be the cause of the accident?

King: Exactly! You have been talked of for a quality wherein they say you shine.

Laertes: What is that, my lord?

King: Why your swordsmanship! Hamlet is so envious of your reputation that he would welcome a chance to fence with you.

Laertes: Ay, my lord.

King: Would you be willing to revenge your father's death?

Laertes: Aye, my lord.

King: Good! Keep close within your room. Hamlet shall know you have returned and will praise your excellence at fencing. Then bring you in together and put a wager on your heads. He will not examine the foils, so that with ease or with a little shuffling you may choose the poisoned sword and quickly send Hamlet to his death for your father.

Laertes: I will do it! I'll prepare my sword. I have a poison so deadly that nothing can save the thing from death that it has scratched!

King: Let's further think of this. If this plan should fail 'twere better if we had a second way planned. When you and Hamlet are fencing, hot and dry, he calls for a drink whereupon sipping he shall die, if he by any chance escape your poison thrust. (Enter Queen.) How now, sweet queen!

Queen: One woe doth tread upon another's heel. Laertes, your sister Ophelia has drowned!

Laertes: Drowned! Where?

Queen: She fell in the weeping brook.

Laertes: Alas, then she is drowned!

Queen: Drowned! Drowned!

Laertes: Too much of water hast thou, poor Ophelia, and therefore I forbid my tears.

(Laertes rushes out.)

King: Let's follow, Gertrude. How much I had to do to calm his rage! Now I fear this will start it all over again. There fore, let's follow.

Scene 11: Hall in the Castle a Few Days Later
(Horatio and Hamlet are talking as Osric enters.)

Osric: My Lord Hamlet, I have a message from his majesty.

Hamlet: I will receive it, sir.

Osric: Sir, a young man named Laertes . . .

Hamlet: What of him?

Osric: No doubt you are acquainted with his fame as a swordsman?

Hamlet: I have heard it.

Osric: Well, my lord, the king has said that you are a better swordsman that his Laertes, and has laid a great wager upon your head.

Hamlet: Has he indeed!

Osric: Indeed he has, my lord. He has bet Laertes that in a dozen passes he shall not exceed you three hits.

Hamlet: What's his weapon?

Osric: Rapier and dagger. The king hath wagered six Barbary horses against six French swords.

Hamlet: Sir, if it please his majesty let the foils be brought. I will win for him and I can!

Osric: Your lordship.

(Osric bows and exits.)

Horatio: You will lose this wager, my lord.

Hamlet: I think not. I have been in constant practice and I shall win. But I am ill, here about my heart, about the death of Ophelia.

Horatio: My good lord, I will tell them you are not fit for this match.

Hamlet: No, Horatio . . . let them come!

Scene 12: Throne Room of the Castle—That Afternoon

(Enter King Claudius, Queen Gertrude, Laertes, Hamlet, Horatio, Osric, and all the attendants and guests. When the King and Queen have seated themselves, all the guests sit.)

King: (Placing Laertes' hand in Hamlet's.)
Come, Hamlet, come and take this hand from me.

Hamlet: (To Laertes.)
Give me your pardon, sir. I've done you wrong, but pardon it as you are a gentleman. What I have done, I here proclaim was madness. Was it Hamlet that wronged Laertes? Never Hamlet. It was Hamlet's madness. Sir, forgive me.

Laertes: I am satisfied. I do receive your offer of friendship and will not wrong it.

Hamlet: I embrace it freely and will my uncle's wager frankly play. Give us the foils!

Laertes: Come, one for me!

King: Give them the foils, Osric. Hamlet, you know the wager?

Hamlet: Very well, my lord. Your grace has laid the odds on the weaker side.

King: I do not fear it. I have seen you both.

Laertes: This is too heavy. Let me see another.

Hamlet: This likes me well. Are these foils all of the same length?

Osric: Ay, my good lord.

King: Set the wine on that table. The king shall drink to Hamlet's better health. Give me the cup. Now the king drinks to Hamlet. Come, begin. Begin!

(Hamlet and Laertes face each other as Osric officially commences the match. Hamlet makes the first touch.)

Osric: A hit! A very hit!

King: Stay, give me drink. Hamlet, this pearl is thine. Here's to thy health. Give me the cup!

(King drops the poisoned pearl into the goblet of wine.)

Hamlet: I'll play this bout first. Set it by awhile. Come! (The match begins again. Hamlet touches Laertes again.) Another hit! What say?

Laertes: A touch, a touch I do confess.

King: Our son shall win.

Queen: He's out of breath. Here, Hamlet, take my handkerchief and rub thy brow. The Queen toasts thy fortune, Hamlet.

(The Queen picks up the poisoned goblet.)

King: Gertrude, do not drink.

Queen: I will, my lord. I pray you, pardon me.

King: (Aside.)
It is the poisoned cup. It is too late.

Queen: Come, let me wipe thy face.

Laertes: (Whispering to the King.)
My lord, I'll hit him now, and yet it is almost against my conscience.

Hamlet: Come for the third, Laertes. You but dally. I pray you, do your best.

(Laertes wounds Hamlet with the poison-tipped sword.)

Laertes: I have you now!

(The fight begins in earnest, and Hamlet knocks the poisoned sword from the hand of Laertes. Laertes goes to pick up his sword, but Hamlet steps on it and gives Laertes his unpoisoned sword.

King: Part them. They are incensed!

Hamlet: Nay. Come again!

Osric: Look to the Queen there!

(Hamlet wounds Laertes with the poisoned sword.

Horatio: How is it, my Lord Hamlet?

Osric: How is it with you, Laertes?

Laertes: Why, Osric, I am justly killed with mine own treachery.

Hamlet: How is the Queen?

King: She swoons to see you hurt.

Queen: No . . . No! The drink . . . the drink . . . O my dear Hamlet . . . the drink . . . the drink . . . I am poisoned!

(Queen dies at Hamlet's feet.)

Hamlet: O villainy! Let the doors be locked! Treachery, I'll seek you out!

Laertes: I am he, Hamlet . . . Hamlet, thou art slain. No medicine in the world can do thee good. You'll not live a half hour of life. The poisoned instrument is in thy hand, and I am killed by it. Lo, here I lie never to rise again. Thy mother's poisoned . . . I can speak no more. The King! The King's to blame!

Hamlet: The point poisoned, too! Then, poison, do thy work!

(Hamlet stabs the King with the poisoned foil.)

King: O defend me, friends. I am but hurt!

Hamlet: Here thou villain. Drink this potion. Follow my mother!

(Hamlet pours the poisoned drink down the King's throat. The King dies.)

Laertes: He is justly served! Exchange forgiveness with me, noble Hamlet.

(Laertes dies.)

Hamlet: I am dying, Horatio. Poor mother, good-bye. Horatio, I am dying! Thou livest. Tell them what I did was right!

Horatio: I'll die with thee!

(Horatio attempts to drink from the poisoned cup.)

Hamlet: Give me the cup! If thou didst ever call me friend, live to tell the story! O I die, Horatio. The potent poison quite o'er crows my spirit. The rest is silence!

(Hamlet dies.)

Horatio: Now cracks a noble heart. Good night, sweet prince, and flights of angels sing thee to thy rest!

Macbeth

Introduction

Macbeth is a foolproof play and breeds success on all levels of innocence or sophistication. This play is a thriller, tinged with mystery and fantasy. Respect the mystery and intrigue of the play by keeping the stage dark and gloomy, but with enough light so that shadows will play upon the curtain, the rear wall, the side drapes, and the entire auditorium. With lighting effects you can capture the fog of the heath, the dampness of the castle, and the terrible dread of the planned evil.

Staging

Scene 1
In front of the curtain, the witches converse. When the witches vanish, it is effective to have them push into the curtains and disappear.

Scene 2
The curtains open upon Macbeth's castle. One or two platforms placed on the stage will suffice. Trumpets heralding King Duncan's arrival will heighten the excitement. The part of this scene where Macbeth and Lady Macbeth plan to kill Duncan is a highlight of the play, particularly if it is played at whisper level, but loud enough to be heard. Macbeth and Lady Macbeth can come forward on the stage as close to the audience as possible when they discuss their plans. One dimly lit spotlight focused on their faces will accentuate the drama of their scheme.

Scene 3
Incorporate a few sound effects as Macbeth moves toward King Duncan's room offstage. A steady, slow beat of a subdued bass drum will increase the suspense of the impending doom for the King. When the drum stops its steady, pulsating beat, the deed has been done.

Scene 4
This scene takes place in the woods and can be staged in front of the curtain. The revengers can be wrapped in the curtain ready to pounce upon Banquo and Fleance. The

audience will wait quietly but tensely, hoping Banquo and his son will manage to escape.

Scene 5
The curtain opens to the banquet scene inside the castle. Increase the brightness to indicate the spirit of festivities but lower the lights when Banquo's ghost appears. The controlled actions of the guests, who never see Banquo's ghost, since it is only a figment of Macbeth's guilty conscience, can be a sight to behold.

Scene 6
In this scene, staged in the heath, various spirits appear to Macbeth. To achieve a hollow effect, suggest that actors playing the spirits speak into empty wastepaper baskets.

Scene 7
This sleepwalking scene takes place in Macbeth's castle.

Scene 8
This final scene requires a quick fight between Macbeth and MacDuff in the castle.

Costumes

The costumes should be merely a suggestion of the mood. A cape for Macbeth is enough and a long skirt is fine for Lady Macbeth. Invite the students to make their own swords. Simple staging, simple lighting, and honest acting will carry the play.

Vocabulary

Scene 1
attire
enraptured
fantastical
heath
imperfect
inhabitants
munched
swine
thane
thrice
traitor
withered

Scene 2
banquet
chastise
confident
grief
hither
hostess
impede
knowledge

mortal
plead
rapt
rejoice
virtues

Scene 3
accompany
appalls
applaud
assailable
balm
blotches
bondage
brainsickly
carousing
chamber
clutch
comfort
conceive
consider
contradict
creation
cricket
deed
descended
entry
fury
gild
grooms
inform
innocent
jovial
knell
leisure
liege
lodged
mistress
multitudinous
Neptune
nourisher
portal
presence
prithee
pronounce
quench
ravelled
reckless
refrain
repent
resemble
sacrilegious
scorpions
scotched
shriek
solemn
spite
stirring
summons
thorough
thrifty
treason
unruly
worthy

Scene 4
affair
approaches

Scene 5
absence
attend
attendants
behold
blanched
ceremony
custom
enrage
fie
glare
hearty
infirmity
marrowless
mirth
momentary
offend
peers
regard
ruby
steeped

Scene 6
accursed
caution
deny
eternal
grieve
pernicious
reign

Scene 7
accustomed
actual
agitation
divine
observe
perceive
physician
remembrance
slumbery

Scene 8

endure
fret
fury
harness
hellhound
mocked
petty
signifying
strut
syllable
tyrant
usurper
villain
wrath

Characters

Duncan, King of Scotland
Malcolm, Duncan's older son
Donalbain, Duncan's younger son
Macbeth, Duncan's general
Banquo, Duncan's general
Fleance, Banquo's son
MacDuff, Scottish nobleman
Ross, Scottish nobleman
Lennox, Scottish nobleman
Lady Macbeth, Macbeth's wife
First Witch
Second Witch
Third Witch
Porter
Messenger
Servants
First Revenger
Second Revenger
Third Revenger
First Apparition
Second Apparition
Doctor
Gentlewoman
Guests at the Banquet

Macbeth

Scene 1: A Heath in Scotland
(Three witches enter.)

First Witch: When shall we three meet again, in thunder, lightning, or in rain?

Second Witch: When the hurly-burly's done, when the battle's lost and won.

Third Witch: That will be ere the set of sun.

First Witch: Where has thou been, sister?

Second Witch: Killing swine.

Third Witch: Sister, where thou?

First Witch: A sailor's wife had chestnuts in her lap, and munched, and munched, and munched. "Give me some," said I. "Away with thee," she cried. Her husband is away at sea, and look what I have!

Second Witch: Show me! Show me!

First Witch: I have her husband's thumb, wrecked as homeward he did come.

(A drum is heard off stage.)

Third Witch: A drum! A drum! Macbeth doth come!

All the Witches: The weird sisters, hand in hand, posters of the sea and land. Thus do go about thrice to thine, and thrice to mine, and thrice again to make up nine. Peace! The charm's wound up!

(Enter Macbeth and Banquo.)

Macbeth: So foul and fair a day I have not seen.

(Banquo sees the half-hidden witches.)

Banquo: What are these so withered and so wild in their attire that look not like the inhabitants of the earth and yet are on it? Are you alive? You seem to understand me. You should be women, and yet you have beards!

Macbeth: Speak if you can. What are you?

First Witch: All hail, Macbeth! hail to thee, Thane of Glamis!

Second Witch: All hail, Macbeth! Hail to thee, Thane of Cawdor!

Third Witch: All hail, Macbeth! Thou shalt be king hereafter!

Banquo: In the name of truth, are you fantastical? You greet Macbeth, to me you speak not. If you can look into the seeds of time, and ask which grain will grow and which will not, speak then to me, who neither beg nor fear your pleasures or your hate.

First Witch: Hail!

Second Witch: Hail!

Third Witch: Hail!

(The three witches vanish into the shadows.)

First Witch: Lesser than Macbeth, and greater!

Second Witch: Not so happy, yet much happier!

Third Witch: Thou shalt get kings, though thou be none. So all hail, Macbeth and Banquo!

All the Witches: Banquo and Macbeth, all hail!

Macbeth: Stay, you imperfect speakers, tell me more. By my father's death I know I am Thane of Glamis, but how am I Thane of Cawdor? The Thane of Cawdor lives, and to be king is impossible. To what do you owe this strange intelligence, and why upon this heath do you stand in our way? Speak, I charge you!

Banquo: Where have they vanished?

Macbeth: Into the air as the wind. I wish they had stayed.

(Enter Ross, who kneels before Macbeth.)

Ross: Hail, Thane of Cawdor!

Banquo: Can the devil speak true?

Macbeth: The Thane of Cawdor lives. Why do you address me so?

Ross: The Thane of Cawdor lives, yes. But it has been proven that he is a traitor to Scotland, and what he has lost, the noble Macbeth [illegible]! Macbeth, we wait for thee.

Macbeth: Forgive me, my dull brain was full of many thoughts. Enough . . . let us go meet the king.

Scene 2: Macbeth's Castle at Dunsinane

(Enter messenger.)

Lady Macbeth: What is your message?

Messenger: King Duncan comes here tonight.

Lady Macbeth: You are mad to say this. Is not Macbeth with the king?

Messenger: Macbeth is almost here, my lady.

(Messenger exits.)

Lady Macbeth: I know he brings great news. Come, you spirits, and fill me from top to toe with cruelty. Come, thick night, and cover me with the darkest smoke so my sharp knife see not the wound it makes, nor heaven peep through the blanket of the dark to cry "Stop! Stop!" (Enter Macbeth.) Great Thane of Glamis! Worthy Thane of Cawdor! Greater than both you shall be hereafter!

Macbeth: King Duncan comes here tonight.

Lady Macbeth: And when does he leave?

Macbeth: Tomorrow.

Lady Macbeth: Never shall he see that tomorrow! Your face, Macbeth, is a book where people may read your thoughts. To fool the time, look like the time. Bear welcome in your eye, your hand, your tongue. Look like the innocent flower, but be the serpent under it. King Duncan is coming and must be taken care of . . .

Macbeth: We will speak further about this.

Lady Macbeth: Look up clear. Be confident, and leave all the rest to me.

(Macbeth and Lady Macbeth exit. A sound of trumpets as King Duncan and his group enter.)

King Duncan: This castle hath a pleasant air. It is delicate.

Banquo: I have noticed, your majesty, that the air is quite delicate.

(Enter Lady Macbeth.)

King Duncan: See our gracious hostess. Where is Macbeth? He rode ahead of us. Ah, how he can ride. Fair and noble hostess, we are your guests tonight.

Lady Macbeth: Your servant ever, your majesty.

King Duncan: Give me your hand. Lead me to Macbeth. We love him highly and shall continue to hold him in our esteem. By your leave, hostess.

(All exit into the banquet room off stage. There is much laughter and talking during the banquet as servants enter and exit with large trays of food. Soon Macbeth enters.)

Macbeth: If I am going to kill King Duncan, then it is best that I do it quickly. King Duncan is so good that his virtues will plead like angels. I have no reason to kill him, but only my ambition that drives me on. (Enter Lady Macbeth.) Well? What news?

Lady Macbeth: He has almost finished his supper. Why have you left the banquet room?

Macbeth: Has he asked for me?

Lady Macbeth: You knew he would!

Macbeth: We will go no further in this horrible business. The king has distinguished me of late. He thinks highly of me!

Lady Macbeth: Are you afraid?

Macbeth: Peace! I dare do all that any man would do. Who dares do more is none!

Lady Macbeth: Then what made you break this agreement with me?

Macbeth: Suppose we fail?

Lady Macbeth: We fail. Screw your courage to the sticking place and we will not fail. When King Duncan is asleep, his two servants will I make drunk with wine. When they are asleep, why cannot you and I attack the unguarded Duncan? We can make it look like the two servants are the ones with guilt. Who will dare question us? We will make our grief roar above his death. Come, Macbeth.

(Lady Macbeth exits.)

Macbeth: False face must hide what the false heart doth know!

(Macbeth exits. The King and his procession retire for the night.)

Scene 3: Macbeth's Castle Two Hours Later
(Banquo and Fleance enter with torches.)

Banquo: How goes the night, boy?

Fleance: The moon is down. I have not heard the clock.

Banquo: Here, take my sword. The heavens are thrifty tonight. Their candles are all out. (Enter Macbeth and a servant.) Give me my sword. Who's there?

Macbeth: A friend.

Banquo: What, sir, not yet at rest? The king's abed. He hath been in unusual pleasure, and sent forth this diamond for your wife. I dreamt last night of three weird sisters. To you they showed some truth.

Macbeth: When we can find the time, let's talk about business.

Banquo: At your kindest leisure.

Macbeth: Good night then, and sleep well.

Banquo: Thanks, sir, the same to you.

(Banquo exits with Fleance.)

Macbeth: (To servant.)
Go bid my mistress, when my drink is ready, she strike upon the bell. Get thee to bed. (Exit servant.) Is this a dagger which I see before me, the handle toward my hand? Come, let me clutch thee. I have thee not, and yet I

see thee still. Art thou but a dagger of the mind, a false creation of my brain? I see thee still, and on thy blade spots of blood which was not so before. There's no such thing! (A bell rings from within.) I go, and it is done. The bell invites me. Hear it not, Duncan, for it is a death knell that summons thee to heaven or to hell.

(Macbeth exits to kill King Duncan. Enter Lady Macbeth.)

Lady Macbeth: That which hath made them drunk hath made them bold. What hath quenched them hath given them fire. Hark! Listen! It was the owl that shrieked. He is about to do the deed. The doors are open, and the grooms are drunk and snoring. I have drugged their wine.

Macbeth: (Within.)
Who's there?

Lady Macbeth: Alas, I am afraid they have awakened! And 'tis not done! I laid their daggers ready . . . he could not miss them. Had their king not resembled my father as he slept. I'd have done it! (Enter Macbeth.) My husband.

Macbeth: I have done the deed! Did you not hear a noise?

Lady Macbeth: I heard the owl scream and the crickets cry. Did not you speak?

Macbeth: When?

Lady Macbeth: Now.

Macbeth: As I descended?

Lady Macbeth: Ay!

Macbeth: Hark! Who lies in the second chamber?

Lady Macbeth: Donalbain.

Macbeth: (Looking at his hands.)
This is a sorry sight!

Lady Macbeth: A foolish thought, to say a sorry sight!

Macbeth: There's one did laugh in his sleep, and one cried, "Murder," that they did wake each other. I stood and heard them. But they did say their prayers and again to sleep.

Lady Macbeth: There are two lodged together.

Macbeth: One cried, "God bless us," and "Amen," the other, as they had seen me with these hangman's hands. Listening to their fear, I could not say "Amen," when they did say "God bless us!"

Lady Macbeth: Consider it not so deeply.

Macbeth: But wherefore could I not pronounce "Amen?" I had most need of blessing, and "Amen" stuck in my throat!

Lady Macbeth: These deeds must not be thought after these ways. It will make us mad.

Macbeth: I thought I heard a voice cry, "Sleep no more! Macbeth does kill sleep," the innocent sleep, sleep, that knits up the ravelled sleeve of care, balm of hurt minds, chief nourisher in life's feast.

Lady Macbeth: What do you mean?

Macbeth: Still it cried "Sleep no more" to all the house. "Glamis hath killed sleep, and therefore Cawdor shall sleep no more. Macbeth shall sleep no more!"

Lady Macbeth: Who was it that thus cried? Why worthy Thane, you do unbend your noble strength to think so brainsickly of such things. Go get some water and wash this witness from your hands. (She sees the dagger in Macbeth's hand.) Why did you bring these daggers from the place? They must lie there. Go carry them, and place them in the hands of the sleepy grooms.

Macbeth: I'll go no more. I am afraid to think what I have done. I dare not look on it again.

Lady Macbeth: Coward! Give me the daggers! The dead are but as pictures. I'll place the daggers, for it must seem the guilt of the grooms.

(Exit Lady Macbeth. A knock is heard on the castle gate.)

Macbeth: Whence is that knocking? How is it with me that every noise appalls me? What hands are here? Ha! Will all great Neptune's ocean wash this deed clean from my hands? No! This, my hand, will rather make the multitudinous seas of green turn to red!

(Enter Lady Macbeth.)

Lady Macbeth: Now my hands are of your color, but I shame to wear a heart so white. (A knock is heard.) I hear a knocking at the south entry. Retire we to our chamber. A little water clears us of this deed. How easy it is then! (Another knock.) Hark, more knocking. Get on your nightgown lest they call us. Be not lost so poorly in your thoughts.

(Lady Macbeth exits.)

Macbeth: To know my deed, 'twere best not know myself! (Another knock.) Wake Duncan with this knocking . . . I wish thou couldst!

(Exit Macbeth. More knocking is heard at the gate. Enter Porter.)

Porter: Here's a knocking indeed! (A knock is heard again.) Knock, knock, knock! Who's there? (More knocking.) Knock, knock! Never at quiet! Who are you? (More knocking. Porter opens the gate.) I pray you, remember the porter.

(Enter MacDuff and Lennox.)

MacDuff: Was it so late, friend, before you went to bed that you do lie so late?

Porter: Faith, sir, we were carousing till very late.

MacDuff: Is thy master stirring? (Enter Macbeth.) Our knocking has awakened him, for here he comes.

Lennox: Good morrow, noble sir.

Macbeth: Good morrow, both.

MacDuff: Is the king stirring, worthy thane?

Macbeth: Not yet.

MacDuff: He did command me to call on him early. I have almost slipped the hour.

(Exits to awaken King Duncan.)

Lennox: Is the king leaving today?

Macbeth: He is. He did say so.

Lennox: The night has been unruly. Where we were, our chimneys were blown down. Some say the earth was feverish and did shake.

Macbeth: 'Twas a rough night.

Lennox: I cannot remember a worse night, sir.

(Enter MacDuff.)

MacDuff: O horror, horror, horror! Tongue nor heart cannot conceive nor name thee!

Macbeth and Lennox: What is wrong?

MacDuff: A most sacreligious murder!

Macbeth: What is it you say . . . murder?

Lennox: Mean you his majesty?

MacDuff: Approach the chamber, and destroy your sight! Do not bid me speak. See, and then speak yourselves. (Exit Macbeth and Lennox.) Awake! Awake! Ring the alarm bell. Murder and treason! Banquo, Donalbain, Malcolm awake! And look on death itself!

(Trumpet blows or bell rings. Enter Lady Macbeth.)

Lady Macbeth: What's the business that such a hideous trumpet calls to awaken the sleepers of the house? Speak! Speak!

MacDuff: O gentle lady, 'tis not for you to hear what I can speak. (Enter Banquo.) O Banquo, Banquo, our royal master's dead!

Lady Macbeth: Woe! Alas! What, in our house?

Banquo: Dear MacDuff, I prithee, contradict thyself, and say it not so!

(Enter Macbeth and Lennox.)

Macbeth: Had I but died an hour before seeing this sight, I had lived a blessed time.

(Enter Malcolm and Donalbain.)

MacDuff: Your royal father's dead!

Malcolm: At whose hand?

Lennox: Those of his chamber, it seems, had done it. Their daggers we found upon their pillows. No man's life was to be trusted with them.

Macbeth: O yet I do repent me of my fury, that I did kill them.

MacDuff: Wherefore did you so?

Macbeth: Who can be wise at such a moment? No man. Here lay King Duncan, there the evil men who committed the deed! Who could refrain from killing them?

Lady Macbeth: Help me . . . I faint!

MacDuff: Look to the lady!

(Lady Macbeth is assisted off stage.)

Banquo: Let us meet and question this most tragic piece of work to know it further!

Macbeth: We can meet in a hall together.

(All exit except Malcolm and Donalbain.)

Macbeth: What will you do? I'll go to England.

Donalbain: To Ireland, I. Our separated fortune shall keep us both the safer. Where we are there are daggers in men's smiles. We are surely in danger if we stay here.

Macbeth: Yes, our safest way is to run. Therefore to horse, and let us not be dainty of leave taking.

(Malcolm and Donalbain exit. Enter MacDuff and Ross.)

MacDuff: Malcolm and Donalbain, the king's two sons, are stolen away and fled, which puts upon them the suspicion of the deed.

Ross: Then 'tis most likely the crown will fall upon Macbeth.

MacDuff: Yes, Macbeth will be king!

(Exit MacDuff and Ross. Enter Banquo.)

Banquo: Thou hast it now, King Cawdor, Glamis. I fear thou playest most foully for it. But hush, no more.

(Enter Macbeth.)

Macbeth: Tonight we hold a solemn supper, sir, and I'll request your presence.

Banquo: Your highness.

Macbeth: Ride you this afternoon?

Banquo: Ay, my good lord.

Macbeth: Is it far you ride?

Banquo: As far, my lord, as will fill up the time between this and supper.

Macbeth: Be back in time for our feast.

Banquo: My lord, I will.

Macbeth: We hear our cousins are hiding in England and Ireland, not confessing to their cruel deed. But we can talk of that tomorrow. Farewell till you return tonight. Does Fleance go with you?

Banquo: Ay, my good lord.

Macbeth: I wish your horses swiftness and sureness of foot. Fare well.

(Exit Banquo. Macbeth speaks to a servant.) Are those men here?

Servant: They are, my lord, outside the palace gate.

Macbeth: Bring them before me. (Exit servant.) To be thus is nothing, but to be safely thus. Our fears in Banquo stick deep. There is none but he that I do fear. (Enter servant and three revengers.) Now go to the door, and stay there till I call. (Exit servant. To the revengers.) Was it not yesterday we spoke together?

First Revenger: It was, so please your highness.

Macbeth: Well then, now, are you convinced that it is Banquo, and not I, that is your enemy? It is he that keeps you so in bondage. Do you believe it?

First Revenger: We do, my liege.

Macbeth: And stand you ready to free yourselves from this bondage forever?

First Revenger: We are men, my lord.

Second Doer: I am one, my liege, whom the world has treated so poorly that I am reckless what I do to spite the world.

Third Revenger: And I another.

First Revenger: We stand ready, my lord, to perform what you command us.

Macbeth: Remember that I require a clearness in this. I will inform you where to plant yourselves some distance from the palace. You must do a thorough job and leave no rub or blotches in the work. Fleance, his son, will accompany him on his ride. Both father and son must die! Both! (Exit three revengers.) It is finished! Banquo, your soul is in flight. If it find heaven, it must be tonight.

(Enter Lady Macbeth.)

Lady Macbeth: How now, my lord, why do you keep alone?

Macbeth: We have but scotched the snake, not killed it!

Lady Macbeth: Come, my lord, be bright and jovial among your guests tonight.

Macbeth: And so I shall, and so, I pray, be you. But full of scorpions is my mind, dear wife. Thou knowest that Banquo and Fleance live.

Lady Macbeth: There's comfort yet, they are assailable.

Macbeth: There shall be done a dreadful deed.

Lady Macbeth: What's to be done?

Macbeth: Be innocent of the knowledge, dearest, till thou applaud the deed.

Scene 4: A Woods Near the Castle Late in the Afternoon

(Enter three revengers.)

First Revenger: It is nearly dark, and near approaches the subject of our watch.

Second Revenger: Hark, I hear horses.

First Revenger: 'Tis he, Banquo.

Third Revenger: He usually walks from here to the palace gate.

(Banquo and Fleance enter.)

Banquo: (To Fleance.)
It will rain tonight.

First Revenger: Let it come down!

(Revengers stab Banquo.)

Banquo: O treachery! Fly, good Fleance! Fly! Fly!

(Banquo dies as Fleance flees.)

Second Revenger: There's but one down! The son is fled!

Third Revenger: We have lost the best half of the affair.

First Revenger: Let's away, and say how much is done.

(All exit.)

Scene 5: That Evening in the Castle Banquet Hall
(Enter Macbeth, Lady Macbeth, Ross, Lennox, and the attendants for the feast to celebrate the crowning of Macbeth as king. Trumpets sound as they enter.)

Macbeth: Please sit down, but first a hearty welcome.

All the Guests: Your Majesty!

(First revenger appears in doorway. Macbeth goes to him.)

Macbeth: Is he dead?

First Revenger: My lord, I did what you asked me towards Banquo.

Macbeth: Thou art the best!

First Revenger: Most royal sir, Fleance did escape.

Macbeth: Then comes my fit again! I will see you tomorrow.
Begone! (Exit First Revenger.)

Lady Macbeth: My good lord, you do not give good cheer. The feast is growing cold.

(Enter ghost of Banquo and sits in Macbeth's chair.)

Lennox: May it please your highness, sit.

Macbeth: Where is our Banquo? His absence lays blame upon his promise.

Ross: Please it your highness to grace us with your royal company.

Macbeth: The table's full.

Lennox: Here is a place reserved, sir.

Macbeth: Where?

Lennox: Here, my good lord. (Macbeth sees Banquo's ghost.) What is it, your highness?

Macbeth: Which of you has done this?

All the Guests: What, my good lord?

Macbeth: Thou canst not say I did it. Don't shake your head at me!

Ross: Gentlemen, rise. His highness is not well.

Lady Macbeth: Sit, worthy friends, my lord is often thus, and has been from his youth. Pray you, keep your seats. The fit is momentary. He will be well in a moment. If you notice him, you shall offend him. Please eat and regard him not. (To Macbeth.) Are you a man?

Macbeth: Ay, and a bold one that dare look on that which might appall the devil himself.

Lady Macbeth: This is only your imagination. This is the air-drawn dagger which, you said, led you to King Duncan. When all is done, you look but on a chair!

Macbeth: Prithee see, there. Behold, look . . . what say you?

(The ghost of Banquo vanishes.)

Lady Macbeth: Get hold of thy self.

Macbeth: But I saw him!

Lady Macbeth: Fie, for shame!

Macbeth: The time has been that, when the brains were out, the man would die, and there an end. But now they rise again and push us from our chairs.

Lady Macbeth: My worthy lord, your noble friends do miss you.

Macbeth: I do forget. (To guests.) I have a strange infirmity which is nothing serious. Come, love and health to all. Give me some wine, fill full. (Banquo's ghost returns to Macbeth's chair.) I drink to the general joy of the whole table, and to our dear friend Banquo, whom we miss. Would he were here. To him we drink.

All the Guests: To Banquo!

(Macbeth sees Banquo's ghost.)

Macbeth: Quit my sight! Let the earth hide thee! Thy bones are marrowless, thy blood is cold. Thou hast no speculation in those eyes which thou dost glare with.

Lady Macbeth: Think of this, good peers, but as a thing of custom. Only it spoils the pleasure of the time.

Macbeth: What any man dare, I dare! Take any shape but this, and my firm nerves shall never tremble. Away horrible shadow! (Banquo's ghost vanishes.) It is gone! I am a man again. Pray you, sit still!

Lady Macbeth: You have displaced the mirth, broke the good meeting.

Macbeth: How can you behold such sights and keep the natural ruby of your cheeks, when mine is blanched with fear?

Ross: What sights, my lord?

Lady Macbeth: I pray you, speak not. He grows worse and worse. Questions enrage him. At once, good night. Don't stand on ceremony, but go at once.

Lennox: Good night and better health attend his majesty.

Lady Macbeth: A kind good night to all.

(All exit except Macbeth and Lady Macbeth.)

Macbeth: What is the hour of the night?

Lady Macbeth: It is almost morning.

Macbeth: Why do you think MacDuff did not come?

Lady Macbeth: Did you send for him?

Macbeth: No, but I've heard it said he would not come, but I will send for him. In his home I keep a spy. Tomorrow I will know the worst for mine own good.

Lady Macbeth: You need sleep, my lord.

Macbeth: Come, to sleep if my strange fear will allow me to sleep.

Scene 6: The Heath the Following Night
(The three witches are dancing around a cauldron.)

First Witch: Thrice the black cat has mewed.

Second Witch: Thrice and once the hedge-hog whined.

Third Witch: 'Tis time, 'tis time.

First Witch: Round about the cauldron go . . . in the poisoned entrails throw.

All the Witches: Double, double toil and trouble . . . fire burn and cauldron bubble.

Second Witch: Fillet of a fenny snake, in the cauldron boil and bake.

Third Witch: Eye of newt and toe of frog, wool of bat and tongue of dog, adder's fork and blind worm's sting, lizard's leg and owlet's wing, for a charm of powerful trouble, like a hell broth boil and bubble.

All the Witches: Cool it with a baboon's blood, then the charm is firm and good.

First Witch: By the picking of my thumbs, something wicked this way comes.

(Enter Macbeth.)

Macbeth: How now, you secret, midnight hags. What is it you do?

All the Witches: A deed without a name.

Macbeth: Answer me to what I ask!

First Witch: Speak!

Second Witch: Demand!

Third Witch: We'll answer!

First Witch: Would you rather hear it from our mouths, or from our masters?

Macbeth: Call them, let me see them!

All the Witches: Come, high or low, thyself to show!

First Spirit: Macbeth! Macbeth! Macbeth! Beware MacDuff!

Macbeth: Whatever thou art, for thy good caution, thanks. MacDuff, thou shalt not live.

All the Witches: Listen, but speak not to it!

Second Spirit: Be brave and proud for Macbeth shall never vanquished be until Great Birnam Wood shall move to high Dunsinane Hill!

Macbeth: That will never be, for how can a forest move its earth bound roots! Yet my heart throbs to know one thing. Tell me, if your art can tell so much, shall Banquo's children ever reign in this kingdom?

All the Witches: Seek to know more!

Second Spirit: Seek to know no more!

Macbeth: I will be satisfied! Deny me this and an eternal curse fall on you!

First Witch: Show!

Second Witch: Show!

Third Witch: Show!

All the Witches: Show his eyes and grieve his heart. Come like shadows, so depart.

(Ghost of Banquo appears with a crown on his head.)

Macbeth: Thou art like the spirit of Banquo! Down! Thy crown doth sear my eyeballs. Why do you show me this? I'll see no more! Horrible sight! (The three witches vanish.) Where are they? Gone! Let this pernicious hour stand accursed in the calendar! Servant!

(Servant enters.)

Servant: What is your grace's will?

Macbeth: Saw you the weird sisters?

Servant: No, my lord.

Macbeth: Came they not by you?

Servant: No indeed, my lord.

Macbeth: I heard the galloping horses. Who was it came by?

Servant: 'Tis two or three, my lord, that bring you word that MacDuff is fled to England.

Macbeth: Fled to England?

Servant: Ay, my good lord.

Macbeth: The castle of MacDuff I will surprise and do away with all unfortunate souls that trace him in his line. This deed I'll do before this purpose cool. But where are these gentlemen? Come, bring me where they are.

Scene 7: Several Nights Later in Macbeth's Castle
(The doctor and gentlewoman are standing on one side.)

Doctor: I have two nights watched with you, but cannot perceive any truth in your report. When was it she last walked?

Gentlewoman: Since his majesty went into the field. I have seen her rise from her bed, throw her nightgown upon her, take forth paper, fold it, write upon it, read it, afterwards seal it, and again return to bed yet all this while in a most fast sleep.

Doctor: In this slumbery agitation, besides her walking and other actual performances, what, at any time, have you heard her say?

Gentlewoman: That, sir, which I will not repeat!

Doctor:	You may tell me and you should.
	(Enter Lady Macbeth with candle.)
Gentlewoman:	Lo you, here she comes and, upon my life, fast asleep. Observe her.
Doctor:	How came she by that light?
Gentlewoman:	She has it lit by her continually. 'Tis her command.
Doctor:	Her eyes are open!
Gentlewoman:	Ay, but her senses are shut!
Doctor:	What is it she does now? Look, how she rubs her hands.
Gentlewoman:	It is an accustomed action with her to be washing her hands. I have known her to continue this a quarter of an hour.
Lady Macbeth:	Yet here's a spot!
Doctor:	Hark, she speaks. I will write down what she says to satisfy my remembrance more strongly.
Lady Macbeth:	Out, damned spot, out I say! Who would have thought the king to have so much blood in him!
Doctor:	Do you mark that?
Lady Macbeth:	What, will these hands never be clean?
Doctor:	We have heard what we should not!
Gentlewoman:	She has spoke what she should not, I am sure of that. Heaven knows what she has done!
Doctor:	What a sigh! This disease is beyond my practice.
Lady Macbeth:	Wash your hands, put on your nightgown! Look not so pale. I tell you again, Banquo's buried. He cannot come out of his grave.
Doctor:	Terrible!
Lady Macbeth:	To bed . . . to bed! There's a knocking at the gate! Come! Come! Come! Come! Give me your hand! What's done cannot be undone. To bed, to bed, to bed!

(Lady Macbeth exits.)

Doctor: Will she now to bed?

Gentlewoman: Directly.

Doctor: More needs she the divine than the physician. So good night. I think, but dare not speak!

Gentlewoman: Good night, good doctor.

Scene 8: Macbeth's Castle a Few Weeks Later
(Macbeth is standing on the castle wall.)

Macbeth: Bring me no more reports. Till Birnam Woods move to Dunsinane Castle, Macbeth shall not vanquished be. The heart I bear shall never shake with fear! (Enter servant.) What is it? Where are you going with that goose look?

Servant: There is ten thousand . . .

Macbeth: Geese, villain?

Servant: Soldiers, sir!

Macbeth: Thou lily-livered boy, what soldiers?

Servant: The English soldiers!

Macbeth: Get thy face away! (Lady Macbeth screams within.) What was that noise?

Servant: It was the cry of a woman, my lord.

(Lady Macbeth screams again.)

Macbeth: The scream again!

(Doctor enters.)

Doctor: The Queen, my lord . . . is dead!

Macbeth: Tomorrow, and tomorrow, and tomorrow creeps in this petty pace from day to day, to the last syllable of recorded time and all our yesterdays have lighted fools the way to dusty death. Out, out brief candle! Life's but a walking shadow, a poor player that struts and frets his hour upon the stage, and then is heard no more. It is a tale told by an idiot, full of sound and fury, signifying nothing! (Enter messenger.) What is thy message . . . quickly!

Messenger: I should report what I saw, but know not how to say it.

Macbeth: Well, say it!

Messenger: As I stood my watch upon the hill, I looked toward Birnam Woods, and I thought the wood began to move.

Macbeth: Liar and slave!

Messenger: Let me endure your wrath, if it be not so! Within this three miles you may see it coming! A moving grove!

Macbeth: If thou speakest false, upon the next tree shalt thou hang. "Fear not till Birnam Wood do come to Dunsinane" . . . and now a wood comes toward Dunsinane! Ring the alarm bell! At least we will die with harness on our back.

(Enter MacDuff.)

MacDuff: Turn, turn!

Macbeth: Of all men else I have avoided thee! But get thee back! My soul is too charged with blood of thine already!

MacDuff: I have no words. My voice is in my sword!

Macbeth: I'll not fight with thee!

MacDuff: Then yield, coward, and live to be mocked! We'll have thee painted upon a pole and under it written, "Here may you see the tyrant!"

Macbeth: I will not yield! Lay on, MacDuff, and damned be him that first cries "Hold, enough!"

(MacDuff kills Macbeth. Malcolm and his attendants enter.)

MacDuff: (To Malcolm.)
Hail, king, for so thou art! The time is free. Hail, King of Scotland!

All the Cast: Hail, King of Scotland!

Romeo and Juliet

Introduction

When the names Romeo and Juliet are mentioned, almost everyone thinks of a balcony, love, and kisses but there is so much more to it than the balcony scene. The play vividly depicts the nonsensical folly of feuds and prejudices. It shows how two innocent young people are trapped and destroyed by the foolishness of their parents and their households.

Staging

Prologue
The prologue is important for it sets the tone of the play. Have the children participating in it enter the auditorium via the center or side aisle, single file with candles, black scarves covering their heads and partially covering their faces. As they form a chorus in front of the curtain, the memorable lines they speak immediately involve the audience in the drama. The same procedure at the end of the play is equally effective.

Scene 1
Use the full stage as the market place in Verona.

Scenes 2-3
Scene 2 is a room in the Capulet's house and scene 3 is a street in Verona. Set both scenes in front of the curtain.

Scene 4
The curtain opens to reveal the ballroom of the Capulet's house. Drape large pieces of brilliantly colored cloth from the ceiling. This can be set up while scenes 2 and 3 are being performed in front of the curtain. Encourage children to choreograph the ballroom scene.

Scene 5
This is the famous balcony scene. Have Juliet enter through the center curtains and hold the curtains open so that a light from her bedroom shines on her. Romeo can be in the orchestra pit or stand in an aisle of the auditorium in darkness. Juliet can stand on a box to give her more height.

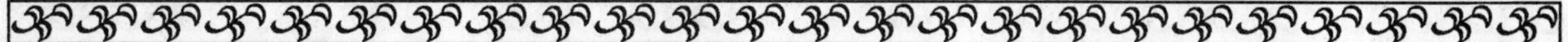

Scene 6
Use the full stage to perform this scene, which takes place on a street in Verona.

Scene 7
Stage this scene of the Capulet's orchard in front of the curtain.

Scene 8
The curtain opens to reveal the market place.

Scene 9
Stage this scene in Juliet's bedroom in front of the curtain.

Scene 10
Friar Lawrence's cell can be set over to one side in front of the curtain. To have Juliet travel from her home to the Friar's cell, she can run around the auditorium and up one aisle on her way.

Scene 11
Play this scene of a hall in the Capulet's house in front of the curtain.

Scene 12
This scene begins in front of the curtain. Then the curtain slightly opens to show Juliet asleep.

Scene 13
Use a dimly lit full stage for this final scene to depict the vault where Juliet is entombed.

Costumes

To help the audience and the cast identify who is a Capulet and who is a Montague, have each Capulet wear blue and each Montague wear gold. To reinforce this identification, hang on one side of the auditorium a large blue shirt with the name "Capulet" beneath it, and on the other side hang a large gold shirt with the name "Montague" written on it. This simple device works well. Of course, there will be various shades of blue and gold in the simple costumes of the actors.

Vocabulary

Prologue
ancient
civil
dignity
grudge
households
mutiny
prologue

Scene 1
cease
forfeit
rebellious
subjects

Scene 2
theme
valiant

Scene 3
pep

Scene 4
depart
doth
enrich
foe
frown
intrusion
kin
yonder

Scene 5
alack
baptized
beseech
changeable
considering
doff
enmity
envious
grief
henceforth
honourable
inconstant
kinsman
peril
purpose
rites
sorrow

Scene 6
courtesy
exception
signor
wager

Scene 7
blushing
compare
fie
jaunt
poultice
weary

Scene 8
affection
amazed
apt
brawl
expressly
fetch
fray
gaze
grievances
livery
mood
mortal
occasion
outrage
plague
pleading
rapier
reputation
retire
shed
slain
slander
slew
submission
surgeon
truce
tutor
unruly
vile
wretched

Scene 9
acknowledge
chamber
comfort
convey
counsel
decision
decree
descend
gallant
match
misty
mumbling
parentage
pity
pomegranate
remedy
tidings
tomb
treason
wretch

Scene 10
borne
distilled
drowsy
liquid
pulse
rouse
testify
thee
vault
vial

Scene 11
beholden
bigamy
dismal
disobedience
friar
henceforth
mixture
repent
reverend
state

Scene 12
corpse
deceased
festival
joints
lamentable
mistress
ordained
revive
untimely
woeful

Scene 13
apothecary
crimson
hence
pardoned
sheath
strife
timeless

Characters

Escalus, Prince of Verona
Lord Montague, head of the Montague household
Lord Capulet, head of the Capulet household
Lady Montague, wife of Lord Montague
Lady Capulet, wife of Lord Capulet
Romeo, son of Lord Montague
Juliet, daughter of Lord Capulet
Mercutio, Romeo's friend
Benvolio, Romeo's friend
Tybalt, Juliet's cousin
Nurse, Juliet's nanny
Friar Lawrence
Servants
Guests
Chorus

Romeo and Juliet

Prologue

Chorus: Two households, both alike in dignity.
In fair Verona where we lay our scene,
From ancient grudge break to new mutiny,
Where civil blood makes civil hands unclean.

Scene 1: The Market Place in Verona
(A crowd of citizens is milling about.)

Citizens: Down with the Capulets! Down with the Montagues!

(The citizens begin to fight each other. Trumpets are sounded as Prince Escalus enters.)

Escalus: Rebellious subjects, enemies to peace, stop this fighting! Cease on pain of torture! Throw your weapons to the ground and hear the sentence of your Prince! Three civil brawls by the Capulets and the Montagues have disturbed the quiet of Verona's streets. If ever you disturb our streets again, your lives shall pay the forfeit of the peace. Now everyone go home! Be gone! Once more, all men depart!

Scene 2: A Room in the Capulet's House

Lady Capulet: Nurse! Nurse! (Nurse enters.) Where's my daughter? Tell her to come to me.

Nurse: I've already told her. Lamb! Lady bird! Where is this girl? Juliet!

(Enter Juliet.)

Juliet: Yes. Who calls?

Nurse: Your mother.

Juliet: Here I am, mother. What is your will?

Lady Capulet: Nurse, leave us alone. We must talk in secret! (Nurse is offended and starts to leave.) Nurse, come back! I'm sorry. You may stay and hear our counsel. You know my daughter's age?

Nurse: Faith, I can tell her age unto the hour.

Lady Capulet: She's not quite fourteen.

Nurse: I'll bet fourteen of my teeth, except I only have four, she's not fourteen.

Lady Capulet: Enough of this. Be quiet.

Juliet: Please, Nurse, be quiet.

Nurse: I'm finished. But you were the prettiest babe that I ever saw. If I could only live to see you married, I'd have my wish.

Lady Capulet: This is the very theme I came to talk about. Tell me, daughter Juliet, how would you like to be married?

Juliet: It is an honour that I hadn't thought about.

Lady Capulet: Well, think of marriage now. Younger girls than you here in Verona are already mothers. Why, I was your mother long before your age. Now, to the point! The valiant Paris seeks you for his wife.

Nurse: A man, young lady! Lady, such a man! He's a handsome man!

Lady Capulet: Please, Nurse! What say you, Juliet? Can you love the gentleman? Tonight you'll see him at our feast. Look him over. Young Paris' face is handsome. Will you try to like him?

Juliet: Yes mother. I'll try.

(Enter servant.)

Servant: Madam, the guests are come. Supper is served. Everyone is asking for you. Please come!

Lady Capulet: We come. (Exit servant.) Come, Juliet.

Nurse: Go, girl. I hope you like him!

Scene 3: A Street in Verona That Evening
(Romeo and his friends are center stage.)

Romeo: I don't know if it's wise for us to go to the Capulet Feast. Besides, I don't feel much like a party.

Benvolio: Hush! We'll hear no more. It's just what you need to pep up your spirit. A few dances and then steal away.

Romeo: O no! I certainly don't feel like dancing.

Mercutio: Romeo, here put on this mask so no one will recognize us as Montagues!

Romeo: It is not wise for us to go, Mercutio.

Mercutio: Don't be foolish. Who will ever know? Everyone will be wearing masks. We will look just like everybody else.

Romeo: I know, but I had a dream. I dreamt that I will come to an early end.

Mercutio: Nonsense. Come along. We shall be too late if you don't hurry.

Romeo: O well, I'll chance it if you will, Mercutio. Lead on!

Benvolio: Let us go!

Scene 4: Later in the Ballroom of the Capulet's House
(As the curtain opens, the guests are dancing.)

Lord Capulet: Welcome, gentlemen, ladies! I have seen the day that I have worn a mask and could tell a whispering tale in a fair lady's ear, but now I'm too old. Come musicians, play! Everybody continue the dance!

Romeo: (Aside to a servant.)
What lady's that which doth enrich the hand of yonder knight?

Servant: I know not, sir.

Romeo: O she doth teach the torches to burn bright. When this dance is done, I'll watch where she goes and follow her. I never saw true beauty until this night.

Tybalt: This, by his voice, should be a Montague. How dare he come here covered with a false face! Now, by the honour of my kin, I'll strike him dead!

Lord Capulet: Tybalt, what is the trouble?

Tybalt: This is a Montague, our foe. A villain that has come here to spite us.

Lord Capulet: Young Romeo, is it?

Tybalt: 'Tis he, that villain Romeo.

Lord Capulet: Calm thee, gentle cousin, let him alone. He's behaving like a gentleman and, to say the truth, Verona brags of him to be a good boy. I would not for the wealth of all this town here in my house do him harm. Therefore be patient, take no note of him. It is my will! Put off these frowns!

Tybalt: I'll not endure it!

Lord Capulet: He shall be endured! I say he shall! Do you hear? Am I the master here, or you? Go, before you make a riot among my guests!

Tybalt: Uncle, 'tis a shame to . . .

Lord Capulet: No more! For shame!

Tybalt: All right, uncle. I will withdraw! But this intrusion shall be paid for!

(Tybalt exits.)

Romeo: (Pointing to Juliet.)

Who is her mother?

Nurse: Why sir, her mother is the lady of the house, and a good lady, too. I nursed her daughter that you ask about. I tell you, he that can marry her shall have the best.

Romeo: Is she a Capulet? O beloved enemy!

Benvolio: Romeo, guests are all leaving.

Lord Capulet: Nay, gentleman, do not depart so soon. There is still plenty of food and drink. What? You will go? Well, then thank you for coming, honest gentlemen and lovely ladies. Good night!

(Exit all but Juliet and Nurse.)

Juliet: Come here, Nurse. Who is the gentleman who just spoke to you?

Nurse: I know not.

Juliet: Go ask his name. (Nurse rushes out.) If he is married, I'll go to my grave unmarried.

(Nurse re-enters.)

Nurse: His name is Romeo, and a Montague, the only son of your greatest enemy.

Juliet: My only love sprung from my only hate. O, that I must love a hated enemy!

Nurse: What's this, what's this?

Juliet: Nothing, nurse.

Nurse: Well, let's go to bed. The guests are gone!

Scene 5: The Capulet's Garden Outside Juliet's Bedroom
Still Later That Evening.
(The balcony scene—Romeo is in the garden when Juliet appears.)

Romeo: But soft, what light through yonder window breaks? It is the east, and Juliet is the sun! Arise, fair sun, and kill the envious moon. See how she leans her cheek upon her hand. O that I were a glove upon that hand, that I might touch that cheek.

Juliet: Ay, me!

Romeo: She speaks! O, speak again, bright angel!

Juliet: O Romeo, Romeo! Why art thou called Romeo? Deny thy father and refuse thy name, or if thou wilt not, be but sworn my love, and I'll no longer be a Capulet.

Romeo: Shall I hear more, or shall I speak at this?

Juliet: 'Tis only thy name that is my enemy. O, be some other name. What's in a name? That which we call a rose by any other name would smell as sweet. Romeo, doff thy name, and for that name, which is no part of thee, take all myself.

Romeo: I take thee at thy word. Call me but love, and I'll be new baptized; henceforth I never will be Romeo.

Juliet: Who is that? Who are you?

Romeo: I know not how to tell thee who I am. My name, dear saint, is hateful to myself, because it is an enemy to thee.

Juliet: My ears have not heard yet a hundred words of thy voice, yet I know the sound. Art thou not Romeo, and a Montague?

Romeo: Neither, fair maid, if either thee dislike.

Juliet: How camest thou here, tell me, and why? The orchard walls are high and hard to climb, and the place death, considering who thou art, if any of my kinsmen find thee here.

Romeo: With love's light wings did I fly over the walls. For stone walls cannot hold love out, and therefore thy kinsmen are no stop to me.

Juliet: If they do see thee, they will kill thee!

Romeo: Alack, there lies more peril in thine eyes than twenty of their swords. Look thou but sweet, and I am proof against their enmity.

Juliet: I would not for the world they saw thee here.

Romeo: I have night's cloak to hide me from their eyes.

Juliet: O gentle Romeo, if thou dost love me, pronounce it faithfully.

Romeo: Lady, by yonder blessed moon I vow.

Juliet: O, swear not by the moon, the inconstant moon that changes every month in the year, lest thy love prove likewise changeable.

Romeo: What shall I swear by?

Juliet: Do not swear at all, and I'll believe thee. A sweet good night!

Nurse: (From within.)
Juliet!

Juliet: I hear some noise from within. Dear love, goodbye. A moment, good Nurse. Sweet Montague, be true! Stay but a little, I will come again.

(Juliet exits.)

Romeo: O blessed, blessed night! I am afraid all this is but a dream! (Re-enter Juliet.)

Juliet: Three words, dear Romeo, and good night indeed. If thy love be honourable, thy purpose marriage, send me word tomorrow by messenger that I'll send to thee, where and what time thou wilt perform the rites, and all my fortunes at they foot I'll lay, and follow thee my lord throughout the world.

Nurse: (From within.)
Juliet!

Juliet: I come, anon. But if thou meanest not well, I do beseech thee . . .

Nurse: (From within.)
Juliet!

Juliet: By and by I come. Leave me to my grief. Tomorrow I will send a messenger. A thousand times good night. (Exit Juliet and re-enter Juliet.) Hist, Romeo! Hist, Romeo!

Romeo: Yes?

Juliet: At what time tomorrow shall I send my messenger to thee?

Romeo: By the hour of nine.

Juliet: I will not fail. 'Tis almost morning, you must go. Good night, good night! Parting is such sweet sorrow that I shall say good night till it be morrow.

(Juliet exits.)

Romeo: Sleep dwell upon thine eyes.

Scene 6: A Street in Verona the Next Morning
(Mercutio and Benvolio are talking.)

Mercutio: Where the devil is this Romeo? Came he not home last night?

Benvolio: Not to his father's. I spoke with his servant. Tybalt, the kinsman to old Capulet, hath sent a letter to his father's house.

Mercutio: I'll wager it's a challenge to a duel.

Benvolio: If it is, Romeo will accept the challenge.

Mercutio: Alas, poor Romeo, then he's already dead. He's no match for Tybalt!

Benvolio: Why not? Why, what is Tybalt?

Mercutio: More than the Prince of Cats, I can tell you. Why he's the best swordsman in Verona with the possible exception of myself.

Benvolio: Here comes Romeo. Good day, Signor Romeo, you gave us the slip last night.

Romeo: Good morrow to you both. Pardon, good Mercutio, my business was great, and in such a case as mine a man may strain courtesy.

Scene 7: The Capulet's Orchard at Noon
(Juliet is alone.)

Juliet: The clock struck nine when I did send my nurse. In half an hour she promised to return. Perhaps she cannot find Romeo . . . that's not so . . . it's noon! And from nine till twelve is three long hours, yet she is not come. O why is she so slow? (Enter Nurse.) O here she comes! O honey nurse, what news? Hast thou met with him? Now, good sweet nurse why do you look so sad? Please tell me.

Nurse: I am weary. Give me a moment. Fie, how my bones ache. What a jaunt have I had!

Juliet: I would thou hadst my bones, and I thy news. Nay, come, I pray thee speak . . . good, good nurse, speak!

Nurse: What haste! Can you not stay awhile? Do you not see that I am out of breath?

Juliet: How art thou out of breath, when thou hast breath to say that thou art out of breath? Is thy news good or bad? Answer me to that. Let me be satisfied. Is it good or bad?

Nurse: Well, you have made a simple choice. You know not how to choose a man. Romeo? No, not he, though his face be better than any man's, and for his figure, it is past compare. He is as gentle as a lamb. Have you dined yet?

Juliet: No, no . . . but all this did I know before. What says he of our marriage? What of that?

Nurse: Heavens, how my head aches! What a head have I! It beats as it would fall in twenty pieces. O, scratch my back . . . the other side. . . ah, my back . . . my back!

Juliet: Sweet, sweet, sweet nurse, tell me, what says my love?

Nurse: Your love says, like an honest gentleman—where is your mother?

Juliet: Where is my mother? Why, she is within, where should she be? How oddly thou repliest. "Your love says, like an honest gentleman, where is your mother?"

Nurse: Are you impatient, dear lady? Is this the poultice for my aching bones? After this, you can deliver your messages yourself!

Juliet: Please, what says Romeo?

Nurse: Have you permission to go to church today?

Juliet: I have.

Nurse: Then quickly to the cell of Friar Lawrence. There stays a husband to make you a wife. Now you're blushing! Quickly to the church. I'll go to dinner. You go to your Romeo.

Juliet: Honest nurse, farewell!

(Juliet kisses Nurse and leaves.)

Scene 8: The Market Place That Afternoon

Benvolio: I pray thee, good Mercutio, let's retire. The day is hot, the Capulets abroad, and if we meet, we shall not escape a brawl, for these hot days put people in a bad mood.

Mercutio: Come, come . . . thou art as hotheaded as any man in Italy, and as soon moved to be moody. And yet thou wilt tutor me from quarrelling?

(Enter Tybalt.)

Benvolio: By my head, here comes Tybalt of the Capulets.

Mercutio: By my heel, I care not!

Tybalt: A word with one of you.

Mercutio: But one word with one of us? Couple it with something. Make it a word and a blow.

Tybalt: You shall find me apt enough to that, sir, if you will give me occasion. Mercutio, where is Romeo?

Mercutio: And what business is that of yours?

Benvolio: We talk here in a public place. Either withdraw unto some private place, or reason coldly of your grievances, or else depart. Here all eyes gaze on us.

Mercutio: Men's eyes were meant to look, and let them gaze. I will not budge for no man's pleasure.

(Enter Romeo.)

Tybalt: Well, peace be with you, sir, here comes my man.

Mercutio: I'll be hanged, sir, if he wears your livery. Therefore he is not your man!

Tybalt: Romeo, thou art a villain.

Romeo: Tybalt, the reason that I have to love thee doth much excuse such a greeting. Villain am I none. Therefore fare well, I see thou knowest me not!

Tybalt: Boy, this shall not excuse the injuries that thou hast done me, therefore turn and draw.

Romeo: I do protest. I never injured thee, but love thee better than thou canst know. Till thou shalt know the reason of my love, good Capulet, be satisfied.

Mercutio: O dishonorable Romeo, vile submission. (Draws sword.) Tybalt, you rat catcher!

Tybalt: What wouldst thou have with me?

Mercutio: Good king of cats, nothing but one of your nine lives. Draw your sword!

Romeo: Gentle Mercutio, put thy rapier up!

Mercutio: Come sir, fight!

(They fight.)

Romeo: Draw, Benvolio, beat down their weapons. Gentlemen, for shame. Stop this outrage. Tybalt! Mercutio! The Prince hath expressly forbid this fighting in the streets. Tybalt! Mercutio! Halt!

(Romeo attempts to stop the fight and in doing so accidentally handicaps Mercutio, at which point Tybalt stabs Mercutio. Tybalt exits quickly.)

Mercutio: I am hurt! A plague on both your houses. I am wounded. Is he gone without a scratch?

Benvolio: Art thou hurt?

Mercutio: Ay, a scratch, but 'tis enough. Go fetch me a surgeon.

Romeo: Courage, Mercutio, the hurt cannot be much.

Mercutio: No, 'tis not so deep as a well, nor so wide as a church door, but 'tis enough . . . 'twill serve. Ask for me tomorrow, and you shall find me in a grave. A plague on both your houses! Why the devil, Romeo, you came between us? I was hurt under your arm.

Romeo: I thought it all for the best.

Mercutio: Help me into some house, Benvolio, or I shall faint. A plague on both your houses!

(Benvolio assists Mercutio off stage.)

Romeo: Mercutio, my very friend, hath got this mortal hurt in my behalf, my reputation stained with Tybalt's slander. . . Tybalt, that an hour hath been my cousin. O sweet Juliet, thy beauty hath made me weak and softened my temper's steel.

(Enter Benvolio.)

Benvolio: O Romeo, Romeo, brave Mercutio is dead!

Romeo: Tybalt shall pay for this with his life.

(Enter Tybalt.)

Benvolio: Here comes the furious Tybalt back again.

Romeo: Alive, in triumph? And Mercutio slain! Now, Tybalt, Mercutio's soul is but a little way above our heads, waiting for thine to keep him company. Either thou, or I, or both must go with him.

Tybalt: Thou wretched boy. You shall join him!

(They fight. Romeo kills Tybalt.)

Benvolio: Romeo, away, be gone! The citizens are up, and Tybalt slain. Don't just stand amazed! The Prince will doom thee to death if thou art caught. Run! Run!

Romeo: I am fortune's fool!

Benvolio: Why dost thou stay! Run!

(Romeo exits. Enter Prince Escalus, Lord Montague, Lord Capulet, Lady Montague, and Lady Capulet.)

Prince: Where are the vile beginners of this fray?

Benvolio: O noble Prince, I can tell you. There lies the man slain by young Romeo, that slew thy kinsman, brave Mercutio.

Lady Capulet: Tybalt, my cousin, my brother's child! What noble blood is spilt! Prince, as thou art true, for blood of ours, shed blood of Montague.

Prince: Benvolio, who began this bloody fray?

Benvolio: Noble Prince, Tybalt began it. Romeo spoke him fair, but he could not make a truce with the unruly Tybalt. He and the bold Mercutio fell to fighting. Romeo attempted to part them, and as he rushed between them, Tybalt underneath his arm thrust his sword and dealt Mercutio a death blow! Then Tybalt fled, but by and by comes back to Romeo, and they go to it like lightning, and before I could part them, Tybalt was slain. As he fell, did Romeo turn and fly. That is the truth, or let Benvolio die!

Lady Capulet: He is a kinsman to the Montague. Affection makes him false. He speaks not true! I beg for justice, which you,

Prince, must give. Romeo slew Tybalt. Romeo must not live!

Prince: Romeo slew Tybalt, Tybalt slew Mercutio. Who now the price of his dear blood doth own?

Lord Montague: Not Romeo, Prince. The law would have taken Tybalt's life for killing Mercutio. Romeo only did what the law would have done.

Prince: And for that offence immediately we do exile Romeo from Verona. I will be deaf to pleadings and excuses. Let Romeo move in haste, else when he is found, that hour is his last. Bear hence this body, and attend our will!

Scene 9: Juliet's Room the Next Morning

Juliet: Wilt thou be gone? It is not yet near day. It was the nightingale, and not the lark. Nightly she sings on yonder pomegranate tree. Believe me, love, it was the nightingale.

Romeo: It was the lark, the herald of the morn, no nightingale. Look, love, night's candles are burnt out, and day stands on tiptoe on the misty mountain tops. I must be gone and live, or stay and die.

Juliet: Then go . . . go! Be gone, away! It is the lark that sings so out of tune. So now be gone . . . more light and light it grows.

Romeo: More light and light, more dark and dark our woes.

(Romeo hides. Nurse enters.)

Nurse: Madam.

Juliet: Nurse?

Nurse: Your lady mother is coming to your chamber. The day is broke. Be wary, look about.

(Nurse exits.)

Juliet: Then, window, let day in, and let life out.

Romeo: Farewell, farewell, I shall descend.

Juliet: I shall be much in years before I see my Romeo again.

Romeo: Farewell, I will omit no opportunity that may convey my greetings to thee.

Juliet: Do you think we will ever meet again?

Romeo: I doubt it not.

Juliet: O my lord, methinks I see thee now as one dead in the bottom of a tomb.

Romeo: Good-bye, my love.

(Romeo exits.)

Juliet: O fortune, fortune, I hope thou wilt not keep him long, but send him back.

Lady Capulet: (From outside.)
Daughter, are you up?

Juliet: Is it my lady mother up so early?

(Enter Lady Capulet.)

Lady Capulet: Why Juliet, what ails thee?

Juliet: Mother, I am not well.

Lady Capulet: Evermore weeping for thy cousin Tybalt's death? Stop crying, and I'll tell thee joyful tidings.

Juliet: Joy comes well in such a needy time. What are they, mother?

Lady Capulet: My child, early next Thursday morning the gallant young Paris at Saint Peter's Church shall happily make thee a joyful bride.

Juliet: He shall not make me a joyful bride. I pray you, tell my father I will not marry yet. These are not good news indeed!

Lady Capulet:	Here comes your father. Tell him yourself, and see how he will take it.
	(Enter Lord Capulet and Nurse.)
Lord Capulet:	How now, what . . . still in tears? Wife, have you delivered to her our decree?
Lady Capulet:	Ay, sir but she says she will not.
Lord Capulet:	What! She will not marry?
Lady Capulet:	She has gone mad! Speak to her.
Juliet:	Good father, I beseech you on my knees, hear me with patience but to speak a word.
Lord Capulet:	Why you disobedient wretch! Get thee to church on Thursday, or never after look me in the face. Speak not, reply not, do not answer me!
Nurse:	God in heaven bless her! You are to blame, my lord, to speak to her like this.
Lord Capulet:	Hold your tongue!
Nurse:	I speak not treason.
Lord Capulet:	Be quiet!
Nurse:	May one not speak?
Lord Capulet:	Peace, you mumbling fool. We do not need your advice.
Lady Capulet:	You are too excited, my lord!
Lord Capulet:	Day and night, that's all I have thought of—to have her matched—and having now provided a gentleman of noble parentage, and then to have her answer, "I'll not wed, I cannot love, I am too young." If you agree with my decision, I'll give you to Paris, but if you do not agree with me, you may hang, beg, starve, die in the streets, and I'll not acknowledge thee!
	(Lord Capulet exits.)

Juliet: Is there no pity that sees my grief? Oh, sweet mother, delay this marriage for a month, a week.

Lady Capulet: Do not talk to me, for I'll not speak a word. Do as thou wilt, for I have done with thee.

(Lady Capulet exits.)

Juliet: O, good Nurse, how shall this be prevented? Comfort me, counsel me. What sayest thou? Hast thou not a word of joy? Some comfort, Nurse!

Nurse: Romeo dare never more return to Verona therefore I think it best you be married to Paris. He's a lovely gentle man. I think you will be happy in this second match.

Juliet: Speakest thou from thy heart?

Nurse: And from my soul, too.

Juliet: Well, thou hast comforted me. Go in and tell my mother that having displeased my father, I have gone to Friar Lawrence's cell to pray for forgiveness.

Nurse: And this is wisely done.

(Nurse exits.)

Juliet: I'll go to the Friar to know his remedy. If all else fails, I shall kill myself.

Scene 10: Later in Friar Lawrence's Cell
(Juliet enters.)

Juliet: O shut the door, and when thou hast done so, come weep with me, past hope, past cure, past help.

Friar Lawrence: Ah, Juliet, I already know thy grief. Thou must on Thursday be married to Paris.

Juliet: Tell me, Friar Lawrence, tell me how I may prevent it. If you cannot help me, I shall use this knife on my heart before I forget Romeo and turn to another. Be not so long to speak. I long to die!

Friar Lawrence: Hold, daughter. I do spy a kind of hope. If thou darest, I'll give thee the remedy.

Juliet: No matter what it is, rather than marry Paris, I will do it without fear or doubt.

Friar Lawrence: Tomorrow night be sure you are alone. Let not thy Nurse lie with thee in the chamber. Take this vial, being then in bed, and drink this distilled liquid. Presently through all thy veins shall run a cold and drowsy feeling. Your pulse will cease, no warmth, no breath shall testify thou livest. The roses in thy cheeks and lips shall fade, thy eyes will close like death. And in this borrowed likeness of death, thou shalt continue two and forty hours, and then awake as from a pleasant sleep. Now, when the bridegroom in the morning comes to rouse thee from thy bed, there thou are dead. Thou shalt be borne to that same ancient vault where all the Capulets lie. You are not afraid to do it?

Juliet: Give it to me. Speak to me not of fear!

Friar Lawrence: Get you gone, be strong.

Juliet: O God, give me strength. Farewell, dear Friar!

Scene 11: Later in a Hall in the Capulet's House

Lord Capulet: What, is my daughter gone to Friar Lawrence?

Nurse: Yes, my lord.

Lord Capulet: Well, I hope he can talk some sense into her.

(Enter Juliet.)

Nurse: See, where she comes with a merry look.

Lord Capulet: Juliet, where have you been?

Juliet: Where I have learned to repent the sin of disobedience. Friar Lawrence has told me to beg your pardon. (Kneels before her father.) Pardon, I beseech you. Henceforth I am ever ruled by you.

Lord Capulet: This holy reverend friar is a wise man, and I am beholden to him. Stand up! This is as it should be! I will myself go to gentle Paris and tell him the good news. We shall have the wedding tomorrow.

Lady Capulet: No, not till Thursday. There is time enough!

Lord Capulet: Tomorrow, I say!

(Exit Lord and Lady Capulet.)

Juliet: Gentle nurse, I pray thee leave me to myself tonight for I have need of many prayers to move the heavens to smile upon my state.

(Enter Lady Capulet.)

Lady Capulet: Need you my help?

Juliet: No, mother, we are prepared for tomorrow. So please you, let me be left alone, and let the nurse this night sit up with you, for I am sure you have your hands full in this so sudden business.

Lady Capulet: Good night. Get thee to bed and rest for thou hast need. (Exit Lady Capulet and Nurse.)

Juliet: Farewell, God knows when we shall meet again. A cold fear thrills through my veins that almost freezes up the heat of life. I'll call them back again to comfort me. Nurse! No! My dismal scene I must act alone. Come vial! What if this mixture does not work at all? What if it is poison that the Friar hath given me to prevent this untold bigamy! No! No! For he is a holy man. Romeo, Romeo, Romeo . . . I drink to thee.

Scene 12: The Next Morning, Capulet's House

Lord Capulet: Heavens, 'tis day already. Count Paris will be here soon, for so he said he would. Nurse! Wife! Ho! Nurse, I say! (Enter Nurse.) Go awaken Juliet, go and trim her up. I'll go and chat with Paris. Make haste, make haste, the bridegroom is already here. Make haste I say!

(Nurse draws curtain to Juliet's bedroom.)

Nurse: Mistress! Mistress! Mistress Juliet! Fast asleep, I warrant. Lamb, Lady Juliet, bride! What, not a word? How soundly she sleeps. I must wake her. Juliet! Juliet! Dressed and asleep! I have to wake you. (Shakes Juliet.) Alas, alas! Help, help! My Juliet's dead . . . My Lord Capulet . . .my Lady Capulet . . .

(Enter Lady Capulet.)

Lady Capulet: What noise is here?

Nurse: O lamentable day!

Lady Capulet: What is the matter?

Nurse: Look . . . look . . . O heavy day!

Lady Capulet: My child, my only life. Revive, look up, or I will die with thee. Help! Help! Help! Call help!

(Enter Lord Capulet.)

Lord Capulet: For shame, bring Juliet forth. Count Paris is here!

Nurse: She's dead, deceased! Alack the day!

Lady Capulet: She's dead, she's dead!

Lord Capulet: Let me see her. Her blood is cold, and her joints are stiff. Death lies on her like an untimely frost upon the sweetest flower of all the field.

Nurse: O lamentable day!

Lady Capulet: O woeful time!

Lord Capulet: Death that hath taken her hence ties up my tongue and will not let me speak.

(Enter Friar Lawrence.)

Friar Lawrence: Come, is the bride ready to go to church?

Lord Capulet: Ready to go, but never to return. The night before her wedding day hath death taken the wife.

Nurse: Oh, woeful, woeful day. Most woeful day that ever, ever, I did behold. Never was seen so black a day as this!

Lord Capulet: Everything that we ordained festival, turn from their office to black funeral.

Friar Lawrence: Everyone prepare to follow this fair corpse unto her grave.

Scene 13: The Next Night in the Tomb of the Capulets
(Romeo is beside the laid out body of Juliet.)

Romeo: O my love, my wife! Death hath no power yet upon thy beauty. Thy lips and cheeks are still crimson. Ah, dear Juliet, I will stay with thee and never depart again. Here, here will I remain. Come poison, go with me to Juliet! (Romeo drinks the poison.) O true apothecary, thy drugs are quick!

(Romeo dies. Juliet awakens.)

Juliet: What's here? A cup closed in my true love's hand? Poison, I see, hath been his timeless end. He has drunk all and left no friendly drop for me. (Juliet sees Romeo's dagger.) O happy dagger, this is thy sheath. (Stabs herself.) Let me die!

(Enter Chorus.)

Chorus: A pair of star-crossed lovers take their life
And with their death bury their parent's strife.
Go hence, to have more talk of these sad things;
Some shall be pardoned and some punished.
For never was a story of more woe
Than this of Juliet and her Romeo.

A Midsummer Night's Dream

Introduction

A Midsummer Night's Dream has a wonderful combination of fantasy, foolishness, and fun. Everyone in the play is a little moonstruck. The magic of King Oberon's forest stimulates creative play among the imaginative minds of children. King Oberon, Queen Titania, Puck, and all the fairies, elves, sprites, and goblins offer endless possibilities for young actors.

The lovers (Demetrius, Helena, Lysander, and Hermia) are vital to the comic flow of the drama, and, here again, the children can utilize their own sense of horseplay.

This play provides a fine opportunity to develop all types of dances for the fairies of the forest. Encourage the actors to begin their creative dancing simply by running about the stage. Eventually patterns and movements will develop. The children can compose their own fairy music with mass humming, or you can play Mendelsohn's Midsummer Night's Dream Overture. When Bottom sings, he can make up a tra-la-la-la song or imitate a rollicking operatic aria.

Staging

Scene 1
This scene takes place in the palace of Theseus and should be staged in front of the curtain. Egeus can "drag" his daughter down the center or side aisle to present his problem to the ruler, Theseus.

Scene 2
The curtain opens upon the magic forest. Except for the opening scene, all the action takes place in the magic forest. A feeling of a magical forest is very important to the play. Consider making a cloth forest. Fasten tree-shaped pieces of cloth against the surrounding drapes or walls. Or, scatter and hang actual tree branches. Encourage children to make suggestions. Children will have many ideas if they are given the chance to think and build.

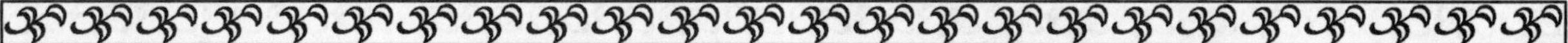

Scene 3
This scene takes place in the same forest the following night. Rather than closing the curtains between scenes, empty the stage of actors to indicate a short passage of time. This scene is a great time to present the fairies of the forest in an opening dance. The forest lighting when the King and Queen are present should always be mysterious in quality, with lots of dancing shadows.

Scene 4
A bower can be wheeled in for Queen Titania, two "trees" can be place together, or two little fairies can hold long branches to represent a bower.

Scene 5
Encourage Queen Titania to show much affection to the donkey's face. The audience will love it. The Queen and Bottom should move up as close to the audience as possible as Titania whispers sweet nothings into the big, long ears.

Scene 6
In this scene there is much running about the stage as the two sets of lovers pursue and flee from each other. Encourage actors to use a lot of holding, pulling, and pushing as they choreograph their movements.

Scene 7
Again, encourage Queen Titania to make exaggerated movements as she shows her affection.

Scene 8
In this scene, you will be staging a play within a play. Position the royal persons and the lovers sitting comfortably at the back of the stage to watch the performance of the amateur actors. The rustics presenting the play introduce themselves to the real audience and present their play to them. For the finale, close the curtains as Puck steps forward to speak the epilogue. After the epilogue, open the curtain slowly on a very dimly lit stage where the fairies of the forest are dancing. After a few moments close the curtains again.

Costumes

Costumes for the creatures of the magic forest should be delicate scarves and capes. Any type of lightweight, sheer fabric can readily establish a magical mood. Actors can wave strips of chiffon as wands. When King Oberon wants to indicate that he is invisible, he can cross his arms in front of his face or partially cover his face with his cloak.

The mortals in the play can wear three-quarter length tunics with a belt around the waist. The royal entourage can wear capes, with the girls in long dresses. Encourage children to create their own donkey head using paper maché.

Vocabulary

Scene 1
abjure
adieu
bewitched
consent
cunning
dispose
elope
endure
entreat
forth
merriment
nosegays
nunnery
pomp
prosecute
pursue
renown
revels
sweetmeats
tokens
vexation
wanes
woo

Scene 2
aggravate
assure
bellows
dogged
lamentable
monstrous
proceed
proper
scroll
tawny
tyrant

Scene 3
amazed
amend
anoint
brawls
changeling
cowslip
dale
disdainful
dissension
doth
entice
forsworn
garments
girdle
grove
haunts
henchman
herb
knavish
meddling
render
shun
sphere
sprite
spurn
wrath

Scene 4
charm
despised
hedgehog
languish
newt
offence
peril
perish
raven
vile

Scene 5
abide
acquaintance
assurance
beseech
bower
casement
chamber
comment
cue
device
enthralled
fowl
hail
hawthorn
mistress
mortal
neigh
odious
prologue
transformed
wilt

Scene 6
astray
bedabbled
bond
carcass
compel
confederacy
conspire
constrain
counterfeit
curst
delight
disparage
divine
fray
henceforth
illusion
injurious
keen
latched

loathed
mockery
perceive
pleading
potion
privilege
scorn
shrewd
vixen
woe
yield

Scene 7
amiable
anon
coy
discourse
dotage
dote
eternally
imperfection
musk roses
vision

Scene 8
beauteous
befall
chink
crannied
discharged
ditty
dole
epilogue
furies
grisly
interlude
mantle
mirth
prologue
quake
slumber
tarry
tedious
tolled
tragical
twain
unto

Characters

Theseus, Duke of Athens
Hippolyta, betrothed to Theseus
Egeus, father to Hermia
Lysander, in love with Hermia
Demetrius, in love with Hermia
Hermia, in love with Lysander
Helena, in love with Demetrius
Philostrate, Master of the Revels
Peter Quince, carpenter
Snug, joiner
Nick Bottom, weaver
Francis Flute, bellows mender
Tom Snout, tinker

Robin Starveling, tailor
Oberon, King of the Fairies
Titania, Queen of the Fairies
Puck, sprite
Peaseblossom, young fairy
Cobweb, young fairy
Moth, young fairy
Mustardseed, young fairy
Other fairies attending the King and Queen

A Midsummer Night's Dream

Scene 1: The Palace of Theseus in Athens
(Theseus, Hippolyta, and Philostrate are on stage.)

Theseus: Now, fair Hippolyta, our wedding day draws near. Four happy days bring a new moon, but oh how slow this old moon wanes.

Hippolyta: Four days will quickly pass, four nights will quickly dream away the time. And then the moon, like a silver bow, shall behold our wedding ceremonies.

Theseus: Go, Master of Revels. Stir up the Athenian youth to merriments. Awake the pert and nimble spirit of mirth, and all Athens shall celebrate. Hippolyta, I wooed thee with my sword, but I will wed thee in another key, with pomp, with triumph, and with revelling.

(Enter Egeus and Hermia followed by Lysander and Demetrius. Exit Philostrate.)

Egeus: Happy be Theseus, our renowned Duke.

Theseus: Thanks, good Egeus. What's the news?

Egeus: Full of vexation come I with complaint against my daughter Hermia. Stand forth, Demetrius. My noble lord, this man hath my consent to marry her. Stand forth, Lysander! And my gracious Duke, this man hath bewitched my child. Lysander, thou hast given her love tokens, thou hast by moonlight at her window sung and given her bracelets, rings, nosegays, and sweetmeats. With cunning hast thou stolen my daughter's heart and turned her obedience to stubbornness. And now, my gracious Duke, she will not consent to marry Demetrius. I beg the ancient privilege of Athens—as she is mine, I may dispose of her, which shall be either to this gentle man or to her death, according to our law.

Theseus: What say you Hermia? Demetrius is a worthy gentleman.

Hermia: So is Lysander!

Theseus: He is, but lacking your father's consent, the other must be held the worthier.

Hermia: I would my father looked but with my own eyes.

Theseus: Your eyes must look with his judgement.

Hermia: I do entreat your Grace to pardon me. I am made bold, but may I know the worst that can happen to me if I refuse to wed Demetrius?

Theseus: Either to die the death, or to abjure forever the society of men. Therefore, fair Hermia, question your desires. Can you endure the life of a nun?

Hermia: Yes, I will, my Lord, before I ever marry a man I do not love.

Theseus: Be not hasty, take time to think, and by the new moon either prepare to die for disobedience to your father's will, or else to wed Demetrius, or to join a nunnery.

Demetrius: Relent, sweet Hermia, and, Lysander, yield to my certain right!

Lysander: You have her father's love, Demetrius. Let me have Hermia's. You marry him!

Egeus: Scornful Lysander! True, he hath my love, and what is mine, I my love shall grant him. She is mine, and I give her to Demetrius.

Lysander: I am, my lord, rich as he, my love is more than his, and Hermia loves me! Why should not I then prosecute my right? Demetrius, I'll say to thy face, made love to Helena and won her soul. The sweet lady is madly in love with him.

Theseus: I must confess I have heard about that and meant to speak to Demetrius about it. But, Demetrius, come, and come, Egeus you shall go with me. I have some private matters for you both. For you, fair Hermia, try to see things your father's way. I cannot change the law of Athens. Come, my Hippolyta.

(Exit all but Lysander and Hermia.)

Lysander: How now, my love? Why is your cheek so pale? The course of true love never did run smooth. Listen, Hermia, I have a rich widow aunt and she hath no child. Her house is seven miles away from Athens, and she regards me as her only son. There, gentle Hermia, will I marry thee, and to that place the sharp Athenian law cannot pursue us. Steal out of they father's house tomorrow night, and in the wood outside the town I'll wait for thee. (Enter Helena.) Look, here comes Helena.

Hermia: God speed, fair Helena.

Helena: You call me fair? Demetrius loves you not me.

Hermia: The more I hate him, the more he follows me.

Helena: The more I love him, the more he hates me.

Hermia: Helena, that is no fault of mine.

Helena: None but your beauty. Would that fault were mine!

Hermia: Take comfort. He no more shall see my face. Lysander and I will fly away from this place.

Lysander: Helena, we'll tell you our secret. Tomorrow night we have decided to elope.

Hermia: And in the wood where you and I often played, there my Lysander and myself shall meet, and from Athens turn away our eyes to seek new friends and stranger companies. Farewell, sweet playfellow, pray for us, and good luck grant thee thy Demetrius. Good-bye, Lysander, we must not see each other till morrow at midnight.

Lysander: All right, my Hermia. (Exit Hermia.) Adieu, Helena. I hope Demetrius will learn to love you.

(Lysander exits.)

Helena: O, how happy they are! Throughout Athens I am thought as fair as she. But what of that? Demetrius thinks not so. I will tell him of fair Hermia's flight. Then to the wood will he tomorrow night pursue her, and for this intelligence at least, he'll thank me.

Scene 2: The Magic Forest That Night

(The six Athenian workmen are gathered together.)

Quince: Is all our company here?

Bottom: You'd better call the role.

Quince: Here is the scroll of every man's name, which is thought fit to act in our play before the Duke and Duchess on their wedding night.

Bottom: First, good Peter Quince, say what the play is about, then read the names of the actors, and so grow to a point.

Quince: All right. Our play is "The Most Lamentable Comedy and Most Cruel Death of Pyramus and Thisby."

Bottom: A very good piece of work, I assure you. Now, good Peter Quince, call forth your actors by the scroll.

Quince: Answer as I call you. Nick Bottom, the weaver.

Bottom: Ready. Name what part I am to play, and proceed.

Quince: You, Nick Bottom, are set down for Pyramus.

Bottom: Who is Pyramus? A lover or a tyrant?

Quince: A lover that kills himself for love.

Bottom: I am better in the role of a tyrant. I could play Hercules very well, but I'll also be good as a lover.

Quince: Francis Flute, the bellows mender.

Flute: Here, Peter Quince.

Quince: Flute, you must take Thisby as your role.

Flute: What is Thisby? A wandering knight?

Quince: It is the lady that Pyramus must love.

Flute: Nay, faith, don't make me play a woman. I have a beard coming.

Quince: That doesn't matter. You shall play it in a mask and you may speak as small as you can.

Bottom: If I may hide my face, let me play Thisby, too. I'll speak in a monstrous little voice . . ."Ah, Pyramus my lover dear . . . thy Thisby dear, and lady dear . . .

Quince: No, no. You must play Pyramus. Flute will play Thisby.

Bottom: Well, proceed.

Quince: Robin Starveling, the tailor.

Starveling: Here, Peter Quince.

Quince: Robin Starveling, you must play Thisby's mother. Tom Snout, the tinker?

Snout: Here, Peter Quince.

Quince: You, Pyramus' father . . . myself, Thisby's father. Snug, the joiner, you the lion's part. And I hope here is a play well cast.

Snug: Have you the lion's part written? If you have, give it to me, for I am a slow study.

Quince: You may do it without lines, for it is nothing but roaring.

Bottom: Let me play the lion, too! I will roar that it will do any man's heart good to hear me. I will roar so well that the Duke will say, "Let him roar again, let him roar again."

Quince: If you should do it too terribly, you would so fright the Duchess and the ladies that they would shriek, and that were enough to hang us all.

All: That would hang us all, every mother's son.

Bottom: I grant you, friends, if you should frighten the ladies out of their wits, they would hang us, but I will aggravate my voice so that I will roar you as gently as any kitten.

Quince: You can play no part but Pyramus, for Pyramus is a sweet-faced man, a proper man, a most lovely gentlemanlike man. Therefore, you must play Pyramus.

Bottom: Well, I will undertake it. What beard were I best to play it in?

Quince: Why, whatever you like.

Bottom: I will play it in either your straw color beard, your orange-tawny beard, your purple-in-grain beard, or your yellow beard.

Quince: Masters, here are your parts, and I request you to memorize them by tomorrow night, and meet me in the palace wood a mile without the town, by moonlight. There will we rehearse, for if we meet in the city, we shall be dogged with company. In the meantime, I will draw a list of properties such as our play needs. I pray you, fail me not.

Bottom: We will meet, and there we may rehearse most wonderfully. Take pains, be perfect. Adieu.

Quince: At the Duke's oak we meet.

(All exit.)

Scene 3: The Forest the Following Night
(Puck and fairies enter from opposite sides of stage.)

Puck: How now, spirit, whither wander you?

First Fairy: Over hill, over dale,
Through bush, through brier
Over park, over pale,
Through flood, through fire.
I do wander everywhere,
Swifter than the moon's sphere
And I serve the Fairy Queen.
I must go seek some dewdrops here,
And hang a pearl in every cowslip's ear.
Farewell, I'll be gone,
Our Queen and all her elves come here soon.

Puck: The King doth keep his revels here tonight. Take heed the Queen come not within his sight. For Oberon is full of wrath because she had stolen a lovely boy from an Indian king, and jealous Oberon would have the child, but she withholds the loved boy, crowns him with flowers and makes him all her joy. And now they never meet but they do so fuss, that all their elves hide for fear.

First Fairy: Either I mistake your shape, or else you are that shrewd and knavish sprite called Robin Goodfellow. Are not you he that misleads night wanderers, laughing at their confusion? Those that call you sweet Puck, you do their work and they shall have good luck. Are not you he?

Puck: That's right. I am that merry wanderer of the night. I jest to Oberon and make him smile . . . and here comes Oberon.

First Fairy: And here, my mistress.

(Enter Oberon and Titania from opposite sides.)

Oberon: Ill met by moonlight, proud Titania.

Titania: What? Jealous Oberon? Fairies, let us go. I have forsworn his company.

Oberon: Tarry, rash Titania. Am I not thy lord?

Titania: Then I must be thy lady. Never since the middle summer's spring met we, but with thy brawls thou hast disturbed our sport. Therefore the spring, the summer, the autumn, angry winter change their appearance, and the amazed world knows not which season is which. This is what comes of our dissension. We are the cause.

Oberon: You amend it then. It is your fault. Why should Titania cross her Oberon? I do beg a little changeling boy to be my henchman.

Titania: Set your heart at rest, the fairyland buys not the child of me. His mother was my friend and, for her sake, do I rear up her boy, and I will not part with him.

Oberon: How long within this wood do you intend to stay?

Titania: Perhaps till after Theseus' wedding day. If you will patiently dance in our round and see our moonlight revels, go with us. If not, shun me, and I will spare your haunts.

Oberon: Give me that boy, and I will go with thee.

Titania: Not for thy fairy kingdom. Fairies, away! We shall argue more, if I longer stay.

(Exit Titania and her fairies.)

Oberon: Well, go thy way. Thou shalt be sorry for this. My gentle Puck, come hither. Fetch me *that* flower, the herb I showed thee once. The juice of it on sleeping eyelids laid will make a man or woman fall madly in love with the next live creature that it sees. Fetch me this herb, and be thou here again quickly.

Puck: I'll put a girdle about the earth in forty minutes.

(Puck exits.)

Oberon: Having once this juice, I'll watch Titania when she is asleep and drop the liquor of it in her eyes. The next thing then she, waking, looks upon, be it lion, bear, or meddling monkey, she shall pursue it with the soul of love. And before I take this charm off from her sight, as I can take it with another herb, I'll make her render up her page to me. But who comes here? I am invisible, and I will overhear their conference.

(Enter Demetrius followed by Helena.)

Demetrius: I love thee not; therefore pursue me not. Where is Lysander and fair Hermia? You told me they were stolen unto this wood. Stop following me!

Helena: You draw me like a magnet. Leave your power to draw, and I shall have no power to follow you!

Demetrius: Do I entice you? Or rather do I not in plainest truth tell you I do not, nor I cannot, love you?

Helena: And even for that, do I love you the more. Demetrius, spurn me, neglect me, only let me follow you.

Demetrius: Tempt not too much the hatred of my spirit, for I am sick when I do look at you.

Helena: And I am sick when I look not at you.

Demetrius: You must return to the city, a young girl like you should not be out at night alone.

Helena: It is not night when I do see your face, nor doth this wood lack worlds of company, for you are all the world. Then how can you say I am alone, when all the world is here?

Demetrius: I'll run from thee, and hide, and leave thee to the mercy of the wild beasts.

Helena: The wildest hath not such a heart as you.

Demetrius: I will not stay. Let me go, and don't follow me!

(Demetrius exits.)

Helena: Ay, in the town, in the field, I'll follow thee.

(Helena exits.)

Oberon: Fare thee well, young lady. Before he leaves this grove, thou shalt run from him and he shall seek thy love.
(Enter Puck.)
Hast thou the flower there?

Puck: Ay, there it is.

Oberon: Give it to me. I know a bank where the wild flowers grow. There sleeps Titania, and with juice of this I'll streak her eyes. Take some of it, and seek through this grove. A sweet Athenian lady is in love with a disdainful youth. Anoint his eyes, but do it when the next thing he sees may be the lady. You will know the man by the Athenian garments he hath on.

Puck: Fear not, my lord, your servant shall do so.

(Oberon and Puck exit.)

Scene 4: The Bower of Titania an Hour Later
(Enter Titania and her fairies.)

Titania: Come, now a fairy song. Sing me now asleep, then let me rest.

First Fairy: You spotted snakes, with double tongue,
Thorny hedgehogs, be not seen,
Newts and blind worms do no wrong.
Come not near our Fairy Queen.

Fairy Chorus: Lulla, lulla, lullaby, lulla, lulla, lullaby.

Second Chorus: Weaving spiders come not here,
Away you long-legged spinner, hence!

Beetles black approach not here,
Worm nor snail do no offence.

Fairy Chorus: Lulla, lulla, lullaby, lulla, lulla, lullaby.

Third Fairy: Away, now all is well.

(Exit fairies. Enter Oberon who tiptoes over to Titania and squeezes the flower juice on her eyelids.)

Oberon: What thou seest, when thou dost awake, do it for thy true love take. Love and languish for his sake. Be it cat or bear, leopard, or boar with bristled hair. Wake when some vile thing is near!

(Exit Oberon. Enter Lysander and Hermia.)

Lysander: Fair love, you faint with wandering in the wood, and to tell the truth, I have lost our way. We will rest Hermia, if you think it best.

Hermia: Be it so, Lysander. Find yourself a bed, for I upon this bank will rest my head.

Lysander: One turf shall serve as pillow for us both.

Hermia: No, Lysander, for my sake, my dear, lie further off yet, do not lie so near.

Lysander: All right. Here is my bed. Sleep give thee rest.

Hermia: Good night!

(Enter Puck.)

Puck: Through the forest have I gone, but Athenian found I none on whose eyes I might drop this flower's magic. (Sees Lysander.) Ah! Who is here? Clothes of Athens he doth wear. This is he who, my master said, despised the Athenian maid, and here the maiden sleeping sound. (He squeezes the flower on Lysander's eyelids.) Upon the eyelids I throw all the power this charm doth owe. So, awake when I am gone, for I must now to Oberon.

(Exit Puck. Enter Demetrius and Helena running.)

Helena: Sweet Demetrius, wait!

Demetrius: I charge thee, get away and do not haunt me thus.

Helena: O wilt thou leave me? Do not so.

Demetrius: Stay on thy peril. I along will go.

(Demetrius exits.)

Helena: O, I am out of breath. But who is here? Lysander, on the ground? Dead, or asleep? I see no blood, no wound. Lysander, if you live, good sir, awake.

Lysander: (Awakening.)
And run through fire I will for thy sweet sake. Where is Demetrius? He shall perish on my sword.

Helena: Do not say so, Lysander, say not so. Hermia still loves you. Be content.

Lysander: Content with Hermia? No, not Hermia, but Helena I love. Who will not change a raven for a dove?

Helena: Why do you mock me? When at your hand did I deserve this scorn? Is it not enough that I never can deserve a sweet look from Demetrius? You do me wrong. Fare you well. I thought you of more true gentleness.

(Helena exits.)

Lysander: Helena!

(Lysander chases after Helena.)

Hermia: (Awakening.)
Help me, Lysander, help me! What a dream was here! Lysander, look how I do quake with fear. Lysander! What, out of hearing? Gone? No sound, no word? Alack, where are you? I faint almost with fear. Either death, or you I'll find immediately.

(Hermia exits.)

Scene 5: Same Spot in the Forest a Little Later
(Titania is lying sleep. Enter Quince, Snug, Bottom, Flute, Snout, and Starveling.)

Bottom: Are we all here?

Quince: Here's a marvelous place for our rehearsal. This green plot shall be our stage, this hawthorn bush our dressing room, and we will do it in action as we will do it before our Duke.

Bottom: Peter Quince?

Quince: Yes, Bottom.

Bottom: There are things in this comedy of Pyramus and Thisby that will never please. First, Pyramus must draw a sword to kill himself, which the ladies cannot abide. How answer you that?

Starveling: I believe we must leave the killing out when all is done.

Bottom: I have a device to make all well. Write me a prologue, and let the prologue seem to say we will do no harm with our swords and that Pyramus is not killed indeed. And for better assurance, tell them that I Pyramus am not Pyramus, but Bottom the weaver. This will put them out of fear.

Quince: Well, we will have such a prologue.

Snout: Will not the ladies be afraid of the lion?

Starveling: I'm afraid so.

Bottom: Masters, to bring in a lion among ladies is a most dreadful thing for there is not a more fearful wild fowl than your lion living, and we ought to look into it.

Snout: Therefore, another prologue must tell he is not a lion.

Bottom: Nay, and half his face must be seen through the lion's neck and he himself must speak through saying thus, "Ladies, oh fair ladies, you think I come hither as a lion. No, I am no such thing. I am Snug, the joiner."

Quince: Well, it shall be so. But there are two hard things. . . that is, to bring the moonlight into a chamber, for you know Pyramus and Thisby meet by moonlight.

Snug: Doth the moon shine the night we play our play?

Bottom: A calendar, a calendar! Look in the almanac. Let us see if the moon doth shine.

Quince: Yes, it doth shine that night.

Bottom: Why then, may you leave a casement of the great chamber window where we play open, and the moon may shine in at the casement.

Quince: Ay, or else one must come in with a lantern and say he comes to represent the person of moonshine. Then, there is another thing we must have. We must have a wall in the great chamber, for Pyramus and Thisby, says the story, did talk through the crack of a wall.

Snout: You can never bring in a wall. What say you Bottom?

Bottom: Some man or other must represent the wall, and let him hold his fingers thus, and through the cranny shall Pyramus and Thisby whisper.

Quince: If that may be, then all is well. Come, sit down everybody and rehearse your parts. Pyramus, you begin, and so everyone according to his cue.

(Enter Puck.)

Puck: What have we here, so near the cradle of the Fairy Queen? What? A play in rehearsal? I'll listen, and be an actor, too, perhaps, if I see a cause.

Quince: Speak, Pyramus. Thisby, stand up.

Bottom: Thisby, the flowers of odious savours sweet . . .

Quince: Odours, odours!

Bottom: Odours savours sweet. So hath thy breath, my dearest Thisby sweet. But hark, a voice . . . stay thou but here awhile, and by and by I will to thee appear.

(Bottom exits.)

Puck: (Aside.)
A stranger Pyramus than ever played here.

(Puck exits.)

Flute: Must I speak now?

Quince: Ay, you must. For you must understand he goes but to see a noise that he heard, and is to come again.

Flute: Most radiant Pyramus, most lily-white of hue, as true as truest horse, that yet would never tire, I'll meet thee Pyramus at Ninny's tomb.

Quince: Ninus' tomb, man! Why you must not speak that yet—that you answer to Pyramus. You speak all your parts at once, cues and all. Pyramus enter, your cue is past. It is "never tire."

Flute: O, that yet would never tire.

(Enter Puck and Bottom wearing a donkey's head.)

Bottom: If I were fair, Thisby, I were only thine!

Quince: O monstrous! O strange! We are haunted. Pray masters, fly! Help!

(Exit Quince, Snug, Flute, Snout, and Starveling.)

Puck: I'll follow you. I'll lead you about around, through bog, through bush, through brier. Sometime a horse I'll be, sometime a hound, and neigh and bark at every turn.

(Puck exits.)

Bottom: Why do they run away? This is a trick of theirs to make me afraid.

(Re-enter Snout and Quince.)

Snout: O Bottom, thou art changed. What do I see on thee?

Bottom: What do you see?

Quince: Bless thee, Bottom, bless thee. Thou art transformed!

(Snout and Quince run out.)

Bottom: I see their knavery! This is to make a fool of me, to frighten me if they could. But I will not stir from this place, do what they can. I will walk up and down here, and will sing, that they shall hear that I am not afraid.

(Bottom begins to sing.)

Titania: (Awakening.)
What angel wakes me from my flower bed? (Bottom sings again.) I pray thee, gentle mortal, sing again. Mine ear is much enamoured of thy note. So is mine eye enthralled to

thy shape, and thy beauty doth move me on the first view to swear I love thee.

Bottom: Methinks, mistress, you should have little reason for that. And yet, to say the truth, reason and love keep little company together nowadays.

Titania: Thou art as wise as thou are beautiful.

Bottom: Not so neither, but if I were, I'd get out of this wood.

Titania: Out of this wood do not desire to go. Thou shalt remain here, whether thou wilt nor no. I do love thee, therefore go with me. I'll give thee fairies to attend thee, and they shall sing while thou on pressed flowers do sleep. Peaseblossom, Cobweb, Moth, and Mustardseed!

(Enter four little fairies.)

Peaseblossom: Ready!

Cobweb: And I!

Moth: And I!

Mustardseed: And I!

All: Where shall we go?

Titania: Be courteous to this gentleman. Feed him with apricots and dewberries; the honey bags steal from the bumble bees. Nod to him, elves, and do him courtesies.

Peaseblossom: Hail, mortal.

All: Hail, mortal!

Bottom: What's your name?

Cobweb: Cobweb.

Bottom: I shall desire more of your acquaintance, good Master Cobweb. Your name, honest gentleman?

Peaseblossom: Peaseblossom.

Bottom: I pray you, commend me to Mistress Squash, your mother, and to Master Stringbean, your father. Your name, I beseech you, sir?

Mustardseed: Mustardseed.

Bottom: Good Master Mustardseed. I know you well. You make my eyes water. I desire to know you better, good Master Mustardseed.

Titania: Come, wait upon him. Lead him to my bower, tie up my love's tongue . . . bring him silently.

(All exit.)

Scene 6: Another Part of the Forest a Few Minutes Later

(Enter Oberon.)

Oberon: I wonder if Titania has awakened? (Enter Puck.) Here comes my messenger. How now, mad spirit?

Puck: My mistress with a monster is in love. Near to her bower she was sleeping. A crew of actors were met together to rehearse a play intended for great Theseus' wedding day. The dumbest one of the lot who played Pyramus forsook his scene and entered in the forest where I fixed on his head, the head of a donkey. When the rest saw him, they all ran away. I left sweet Pyramus there when in that moment Titania woke up and immediately fell in love with a donkey.

Oberon: This falls out better than I imagined it would. But hast thou yet latched the Athenian's eyes with the love juice as I told thee to do?

Puck: I did while he was sleeping, and the Athenian woman by his side that, when he waked, by force she must be eyed.

(Enter Hermia and Demetrius.)

Oberon: Stand close, this is the same Athenian.

Puck: This is the woman, but this is not the man.

Demetrius: O, why rebuke me when I love you so?

Hermia: If thou hast slain Lysander in his sleep, plunge in the knife and kill me too. It cannot be that thou hast killed him. Where is my Lysander? Ah, good Demetrius, wilt thou give him to me?

Demetrius: I had rather give his carcass to my hounds.

Hermia: Hast thou slain him, then? Henceforth be never numbered among men. Hast thou killed him sleeping?

Demetrius: No, I am not guilty of Lysander's blood, nor is he dead that I know of.

Hermia: I pray thee, tell me where he is!

Demetrius: And if I could, what should I get for it?

Hermia: A privilege, never to see me more, whether he be dead or no!

(Hermia exits.)

Demetrius: There is no following her in this fierce vein. Here, therefore, for a while I will remain. So sorrow's heaviness doth heavier grow. O, I am sleepy.

(Lies down and sleeps.)

Oberon: (To Puck.)
What hast thou done? Thou hast made a mistake! And laid the love juice on some true love's sight. This is true love turned, and not a false turned true.

Puck: I'm sorry, master. Can we mend it?

Oberon: Go swifter than the wind and find Helena of Athens. She is sick with sighs of love. By some illusion bring her here. I'll charm his eyes till she doth appear.

Puck: I go, I go! Look how I go! Swifter than an arrow from a bow. (Exits.)

Oberon: (Squeezes the flower on Demetrius.)
Flower of this purple dye, sink in the apple of his eyes. When thou wakest, if she be by, thou shalt love her eye to eye.

(Re-enter Puck.)

Puck: Helena is here at hand, and the youth, mistook by me, pleading for her love. Shall we watch? Lord, what fools these mortals be!

Oberon: Stand aside. The noise they make will cause Demetrius to wake.

Puck: Then will both of them love her!

(Much laughter. Enter Helena and Lysander.)

Lysander: Why should you think that I woo in mockery. Look, when I vow, I weep.

Helena: You're making fun of me. You love only Hermia.

Lysander: No, Demetrius loves her, and he loves not you.

Demetrius: (Awakening.)
O Helena, goddess divine! To what, my love, shall I compare thee? O, let me kiss you.

Helena: I see you all are bent on making fun of me for your merriment. How can you treat me this way! You both are rivals and love Hermia, and now both rival to mock Helena.

Lysander: You are unkind, Demetrius, for you love Hermia. This you know I know. And here, with all my heart, in Hermia's love I yield you up my part. I do love Helena and will till death.

Helena: This is monstrous!

Demetrius: Lysander, keep Hermia. If I loved her, all that love is gone. Now I love Helena.

Lysander: Helena, it is not so.

Demetrius: Disparage not my love. Look, here comes thy love. Yonder is thy dear.

(Enter Hermia.)

Hermia: Lysander, why did you leave me so unkindly?

Lysander: Why should I stay, when love doth call me! I love fair Helena! Why do you seek me?

Hermia: You speak not as you think. It cannot be.

Helena: Lo! She is one of this confederacy. Now I perceive they have joined all three to fashion this false sport in spite of me. Injurious Hermia, have you conspired with these men in scorning your poor friend? It is not friendly.

Hermia: I am amazed. I scorn you not. It seems that you scorn me.

Helena: Have you not sent Lysander to follow me and to praise my eyes and face? And made your other love, Demetrius, to call me goddess divine?

Hermia: I understand not. What do you mean by this?

Helena: That's right, keep up the show, counterfeit sad looks. Make faces at me when I turn my back. Wink at each other . . . laugh at me! If you have any pity or manners, you would not tease me so. But fare ye well, 'tis partly mine own fault!

Lysander: Stay, gentle Helena, hear my excuse. My love, my life, my soul, fair Helena.

Helena: Stop it!

Hermia: Sweet, do not tease her so.

Demetrius: If she cannot entreat, I can compel.

Lysander: Thou canst compel me no more than she entreat. Helena, I love thee, by my life, I do.

Demetrius: I say I love thee more than he can do.

Lysander: Then prove it with your sword. Come with me.

Demetrius: Gladly! After you!

Hermia: Lysander, what does this mean?

Lysander: Go ahead, Demetrius!

(Hermia throws her arms around Lysander.)

Demetrius: You are a coward!

Lysander: Coward! (To Hermia.) Take your hands off me, or I will shake thee from me like a serpent.

Hermia: Why are you grown so rude? What change is this, sweet love?

Lysander: Thy love? Out loathed medicine! O hated potion, away.

Hermia: Do you not jest?

Helena: Yes, of course he does, and so do you.

Lysander: Demetrius, I will keep my word with you.

Demetrius: I would I had your bond, for I perceive a weak bond holds you. I'll not trust your word.

Lysander: Why should I hurt her, strike her, kill her dead? Although I hate her, I'll not harm her so.

Hermia: What? Can you do me greater harm than hate? Hate me . . . why? Am I not Hermia? Are you not Lysander? I am as fair now as I was before. Why then you left me on purpose?

Lysander: Yes! And never did desire to see thee more. Therefore, be certain it is not jest that I do hate thee, and love Helena.

Hermia: (To Helena.)
O, you thief of love! You have come by night and stolen my love's heart from him.

Helena: Why, why . . . you counterfeit . . .you puppet, you!

Hermia: Puppet? (Attempts to attack Helena.)

Helena: I pray you, gentlemen, let her not hurt me. Let her not strike me.

Lysander: Be not afraid. She shall not harm thee.

Demetrius: No sir, she shall not.

Helena: When she's angry, she is keen and shrewd. She was a vixen when she went to school, and though she be but little, she is fierce.

Hermia: Why will you let her insult me so? Let me at her!

Lysander: (To Hermia.)
Get you gone, you bead, you acorn!

Demetrius: Who asked you to speak for Helena? Take not her part.

Lysander: Now she holds me not. Now follow, if thy darest. I'll show you who has a right to take up for Helena.

Demetrius: I'll follow thee!

(Exit Lysander and Demetrius.)

Helena: (To Hermia.)
I will not trust you. I no longer stay in your curst company. Your hands than mine are quicker for a fray. My legs are longer though, to run away!

(Helena exits.)

Hermia: I am amazed, and know not what to say!

(Hermia exits.)

Oberon: Is this another mistake? Or did you do this on purpose?

Puck: Believe me, king of shadows, I mistook. Did not you tell me I should know the man by the Athenian garments he had on?

Oberon: Thou seest these lovers seek a place to fight, therefore lead these rivals so astray as one come not within another's way, and put them to sleep. Then crush this herb into Lysander's eye, whose liquid hath this quality to take from thence all error with his sight. When they awake, all this shall seem a dream, and back to Athens shall the lovers go. I'll to my queen and beg her Indian boy, and then I will her charmed eye release from monster's view, and all things shall be peace.

Puck: My fairy lord, this must be done with haste, for night's beauty is nearly over. It will soon be dawn.

Oberon: Make no delay. We may effect this business yet before day. (Exits.)

Puck: Here comes one of them.

(Re-enter Lysander.)

Lysander: Where are thou, proud Demetrius? Speak thou now! The villain is much lighter heeled than I. I followed fast, but faster he did fly. O, I am tired. I'll rest a little then in the morning I'll find Demetrius and achieve my revenge.

(Lysander lies down and sleeps. Re-enter Demetrius.)

Demetrius: Where art thou, Lysander? If ever thy face I see! Faintness constraineth me to measure out my lengths on this cold bed.

(Demetrius lies down and sleeps. Re-enter Helena.)

Helena: O weary night, oh long and tedious night, abate thy hours. Shine comforts from the east, that I may back to Athens by daylight. And sleep, that sometime shuts up sorrow's eye, steal me awhile from mine own company.

(Lies down and sleeps.)

Puck: Yet but three? Come, one more. Two of both kinds make four. Here she comes, curst and sad. Cupid is a knavish lad, thus to make poor females mad.

(Re-enter Hermia.)

Hermia: Never so weary, never so in woe, bedabbled with the dew and torn with briers. I can no further crawl, no further go. My legs can keep no pace with my desires. Here will I rest me till the break of day. Heavens shield Lysander, if they have a fray.

(Lies down and sleeps.)

Puck: On the ground sleep sound. I'll apply to your eye, gentle lover, remedy. (Squeezes the herb on Lysander's eyelids.) When thou wakest, thou takest true delight in the sight of thy former lady's eye. Jack shall have a Jill, naught shall go ill, and all shall be well.

Scene 7: Titania's Bower in the Forest Early the Next Morning

(Enter Titania, Bottom, and the fairies. Oberon is hiding in the background.)

Titania: Come sit thee down upon this flowery bed, while I thy amiable cheeks do coy, and stick muskroses in thy smooth head, and kiss thy fair large ears, my gentle joy.

Bottom: Where's Peaseblossom?

Peaseblossom: Ready.

Bottom: Scratch my head, Peaseblossom. Where is Master Cobweb?

Cobweb: Ready.

Bottom: Where is Master Mustardseed?

Mustardseed: What is your will?

Bottom: Nothing, but to help Peaseblossom and Cobweb to scratch. I must to the barber's, for methinks I am marvellous hairy about the face. And I am such a tender donkey, if one hair do but tickle me, I must scratch.

Titania: Wilt thou hear some music, my sweet love?

Bottom: I have a reasonable good ear in music. Let's have some music.

Titania: Or say, sweet love, what thou desirest to eat.

Bottom: Truly, a peck of good dry oats. Methinks I have a great desire to a bottle of hay.

Titania: I have a venturous fairy that shall seek the squirrel's hoard and fetch thee new nuts.

Bottom: I had rather have a handful or two of dried peas. But, I pray you, let none of your people stir me. I have a feeling of sleep come upon me.

Titania: Sleep thou, and I will wind thee in my arms. Fairies be gone. (Exit all the fairies.) O how I love thee! How I dote on thee!

(They sleep. Oberon steps forward and Puck enters.)

Oberon: Welcome, good Puck. Seest thou this sweet sight? Her dotage now I do begin to pity. For now I have the boy, I will undo this hateful imperfection of her eyes. And, gentle Puck, take this transformed scalp from off the head of this Athenian, that he, awakening when the others do, may all go back to Athens and think of this night's accidents as a merry dream. But first I will release the Fairy Queen. (Touches her eyes with an herb.) Now my Titania, wake you, my sweet Queen.

Titania: My Oberon, what visions have I seen! Me thought I was in love with a donkey!

Oberon: There lies your love!

Titania: (Screaming.)
How came these things to pass? O, how mine eyes do loathe his visage now.

Oberon:	Silence awhile. Puck, take off his head. Titania, music call, to wake these five from their charmed sleep. (Music swells.) Come, my Queen, take hands with me, and rock the ground whereon these sleepers be. We will tomorrow midnight dance in Duke Theseus' house, and there shall the pairs of faithful lovers be wedded with Theseus.
Puck:	Fairy King, attend and mark . . . I do hear the morning lark.
Oberon:	Then, my Queen, trip we after night's shade, swifter than the wandering noon.
Titania:	Come, my lord, and tell me how it came about that I sleeping here was found with these mortals on the ground!
	(Exit Oberon, Titania, and fairies. Enter Theseus and Egeus.)
Egeus:	There they are, my lord. This is my daughter here asleep, and this is Lysander. Enough, my lord. You have seen enough. I beg the law, the law upon his head! (The lovers awake.) They would have stolen away, they would, Demetrius thereby to have defeated you and me.
Demetrius:	But, my lord, I love Helena, and she loves me. My love to Hermia melted as the snow.
Theseus:	Fair lovers, you are fortunately met. Of this discourse we more will hear anon. Egeus, in the temple, by and by, these couples shall be eternally knit. We will hold a feast. Come along everyone.
	(All exit except Bottom.)
Bottom:	(Awakening.) When my cue comes, call me, and I will answer. Heigh ho! Peter Quince? Flute, the bellows mender? Snout, the tinker? Starveling? They stole away and left me asleep. I have had a most rare dream! Methought I was . . . a. . .
	(Runs off.)

Scene 8: Theseus' Palace That Evening
(Enter Hippolyta, Theseus, and Philostrate.)

Hippolyta: 'Tis strange, my Theseus, the story that these lovers told.

Theseus: More strange than true. I never believe these fairy stories. It was only their imaginations. (Enter Lysander, Demetrius, Hermia, and Helena.) Here comes the lovers, full of mirth and joy. Gentle friends, come now. What masks, what dances shall we have? Where is our usual manner of mirth? What revels are in hand? Is there no play?

Philostrate: Here, mighty Theseus, here is a list. Make choice of which your highness will see first.

Theseus: A tedious brief scene of young Pyramus and his love Thisby . . . very tragical mirth? Merry and tragical? Tedious and brief? What are they that do play it?

Philostrate: Hard handed men that work in Athens here.

Theseus: I will hear that play. For never anything can be amiss when simpleness and duty tender it. Go bring them in, and all take your places.

Philostrate: So please your Grace, the prologue is ready.

Theseus: Let him approach.

(Trumpets sound. Enter Quince as the Prologue, Bottom as Pyramus, Flute as Thisby, Snout as the Wall, Starveling as Moonshine, and Snug as the Lion.)

Quince: Ladies and gentlemen, perhaps you wonder at this show but, wonder on, till truth make all things plain. This man is Pyramus, if you would know. This beauteous lady is Thisby. This man doth present a wall, that vile wall, and through the wall's crack, poor souls, they are content to whisper. This man with lantern presenteth Moonshine. For by moonshine did these lovers think to meet at Ninus' tomb, there, there to woo. This grisly beast, Lion by name, the trusty Thisby, coming first by night, did scare away, and as she fled, her mantle she did let fall. Anon comes Pyramus, sweet youth and tall, and finds his trusty Thisby's mantle stained, whereupon with his sword he bravely stabbed himself. And Thisby, tarrying in mulberry shade, his dagger drew and died. For all the rest, let Lion, Moonshine, Wall, and lovers twain, at large discourse while here they do remain.

(Exit Prologue, Pyramus, Thisby, Lion, and Moonshine.)

Theseus: I wonder if the lion will speak?

Wall: In this same interlude it doth befall, that I, one Snout by name, present a wall. And such a wall that had in it a crannied hole or crack, through which the lovers, Pyramus and Thisby, did whisper often very secretly.

(Re-enter Pyramus.)

Theseus: Pyramus draws near the wall.

Pyramus: I fear my Thisby's promise is forgot. And thou O wall, O sweet, O lovely wall that standest between her father's ground and mine, show me thy crack to blink through with my eye. (Wall holds up his fingers.) Thanks, courteous wall. But what see I? No Thisby do I see. O wicked wall, curst be thy stones for thus deceiving me.

Theseus: The wall, methinks, being sensible should curse back at him.

Bottom: No, in truth, sir, he should not. "Deceiving me" is Thisby's cue. She is to enter now, and I am to spy her through the wall. You shall see it will fall pat as I told you. (Enter Thisby.) Yonder she comes.

Thisby: O wall, often hast thou heard my moans for parting my fair Pyramus and me. My cherry lips have often kissed thy stones.

Pyramus: I see a voice . . . now will I to the crack to spy and I can hear my Thisby's face. Thisby?

Thisby: My love thou art, my love I think.

Pyramus: Think what thou wilt, I am thy lover. O kiss me, through the hole of this vile wall.

Thisby: I kiss the wall's hole, not your lips at all.

Pyramus: Wilt thou at Ninny's tomb meet me straightaway?

Thisby: I come without delay.

(Exit Pyramus and Thisby.)

Wall: Thus have I, Wall, my part discharged so and, being done, thus Wall away doth go.

(Exits.)

Hippolyta: This is the silliest stuff that ever I heard.

Theseus: Shush! (Enter Lion and Moonshine.) Here come two noble beasts . . . a moon and a lion.

Lion: Young ladies, you who fear the smallest monstrous mouse that creeps on the floor, do not quake and tremble when Lion doth roar. Then know that I, Snug the joiner, am not really a lion at all.

Theseus: A very gentle beast and of good conscience. Let us listen to the moon.

Moonshine: This lantern doth the moon represent. Myself the man in the moon do seem to be.

Theseus: This is the greatest error of all the rest. The man should be put into the lantern. How is it else the man in the moon?

Moonshine: All that I have to say is to tell you that the lantern is the moon. I the man in the moon.

(Re-enter Thisby.)

Demetrius: Silence, here comes Thisby.

Thisby: This is old Ninny's tomb. Where is my love?

Lion: Roooarrr!

(Thisby runs off.)

Demetrius: Well roared, Lion.

Theseus: Well run, Thisby.

Hippolyta: Well shone, Moon.

(Lion tears Thisby's mantle and exits. Pyramus re-enters.)

Pyramus: Sweet moon, I thank thee for shining now so bright, for by thy gracious golden glittering beams, I trust to take of truest Thisby sight. But stay . . . O spite! What dreadful dole is here? How can it be? Thy mantle stained with blood! Approach ye furies. . . O fates come, come! Crush, conclude!

Theseus: This passion and the death of a good friend would go near to make a man look sad.

Pyramus: Come tears, confound. Out sword and wound the breast of Pyramus . . . that left breast where heart doth hop. (Stabs himself.) Thus die I, thus, thus, thus. Now am I dead. Moon take thy flight. (Exit Moonshine.) Now die, die, die, die, die.

(Pyramus dies.)

Theseus: With the help of a surgeon he might yet recover.

Hippolyta: How chance Moonshine is gone before Thisby comes back and finds her lover?

(Re-enters Thisby.)

Theseus: She will find him by starlight. Here she comes to end the play.

Hippolyta: I hope she will be brief.

Lysander: She hath spied him already with those sweet eyes.

Thisby: Asleep, my love? What, dead, my dove? O Pyramus arise! Speak . . . speak! Quite dumb! Dead, dead? A tomb must cover thy sweet eyes. His eyes were green as leeks. O come trusty sword! (Stabs herself.) And farewell friends, thus Thisby ends. Adieu, adieu, adieu!

(Thisby dies.)

Theseus: Moonshine and Lion are left to bury the dead.

Demetrius: Ay, and the wall, too.

Bottom: (Standing up.)
Will it please you to see the epilogue?

Theseus: No epilogue, I pray you, for your play needs no excuse. Never excuse, for when the players are all dead there need none to be blamed. The iron tongue of midnight hath tolled twelve. Sweet friends, to bed.

(All mortals exit. Enter King Oberon, Queen Titania, and all the fairies.)

Oberon: Through the house give glimmering light, every elf and fairy sprite sing this ditty after me, and dance it trippingly.

Titania: Hand in hand with fairy grace, will we sing, and bless this place.

(Song and dance of fairies.)

Oberon: Trip away, make not stay,
Meet me all by break of day.

(All exit. Enter Puck.)

Puck: If we shadows have offended, think that you but slumbered here while these visions did appear. And as I am an honest Puck, good night unto you all.

Julius Caesar

Introduction

The most impressive feature of *Julius Caesar* is the vitality and energy of the crowd—the citizens of Rome. From the very opening of the play, the crowd is evident as it slowly disperses when threatened by a soldier. Of course, the central characters of Caesar, Brutus, Antony, and Cassius are important, but it is the crowd that gives the play its pulse beat. The violence of the Roman citizenry sweeps through the entire play and absorbs the audience.

The first thing the crowd must learn is that discipline is required to display anger and rage in a controlled way. The crowd must be spontaneous and yet aware that team work is involved. It is extremely important that the children in the crowd understand how important they are and how vital it is for them to remain in character. Once the crowd believes in itself, the play will fall into place very easily.

Staging

Scene 1

Make two signs reading "House of Brutus" and "House of Caesar." Attach one sign to one side of the closed curtain and the other to the opposite side of the curtain. When the audience enters the auditorium, it sees the closed curtain with the two signs in bold view. When the curtain opens, the crowd should be in place, motionless as statues to convey the feeling of taking the audience back in history. This is an appropriate time for the narrator to explain to the audience some of the highlights of the play. The statues come to life when the soldier dismisses them from the area. When Caesar enters from a door or hallway, include a musical fanfare. To add to the mystery and conspiracy of the production, have the soothsayer's voice come from the back of the auditorium in darkness. Provide a platform in the middle of the stage on which Caesar can stand.

Scene 2

With the curtain drawn, have Cassius and Casca enact their encounter on an extreme side of the stage or auditorium. When Casca throws the letter through Brutus' window, he takes a rock that has been placed nearby ahead of time along with a rubber band, wraps the letter around the rock, puts the rubber band around the paper, and hurls the rock at the side of the curtain that says "House of Brutus." Casca then flees into the darkness of the night. When Brutus hears the crash of the rock, he steps from behind the curtain to the front to see what is what. The scene with Brutus, the conspirators, and Portia is staged in front of the curtain. The crowd remains on the side of the curtain that says "House of Brutus." The conspirators can partially cover their faces with their mantles to create a feeling of intrigue.

Scene 3
This scene between Calpurnia and Caesar should be staged in front of a sign that says, "House of Caesar."

Scene 4
This is the scene where the reaction of the citizens to Caesar's death makes the whole play believable. When Caesar is killed, use a slow bass drum beat that increases in intensity.

Scene 5
The give and take between the crowd and Brutus and the crowd and Mark Antony can be excitement personified. When the mob reaches its peak of anger and holds red cellophane-covered torches, the audience will sense the burning of Rome.

Costumes

Sheets, simply draped, are most adequate costumes. Actors can edge their togas with a bit of paint or crayon if they desire. Caesar might can wear a wreath of laurel leaves on his head. Portia and Calpurnia can wear slightly disguised nightgowns.

Adjust the number of conspirators and citizens to accommodate the size of your class.

Vocabulary

Scene 1
avoid
chamber
Colossus
conspirator
endure
Ides of March
influenced
neglected
petty
seldom
senate
soothsayer
throng
Tiber
wretched

Scene 2
brewing
carcass
decision
establish
flatter
hew
oath
oversway
persuasion
physically
purgers
resolution
sighing
superstitious
trustworthy
worthy
wrathfully

Scene 3
apt
bids
concluded
misinterpreted
mock
reviving
signify
spouting
stir
valiant
yield

Scene 4
amazed
ambition
appeased
aside
conquests
consent
curse
debt
devise
Et tu Brute
fled
meek
misgivings
multitude
prophecy
pulpit
tyranny
utter
woe

Scene 5
afoot
ancestors
entreat
arbours
ascended
assembly
base
beholding
benefit
blunt
captives
coffers
compel
course
disprove
drachmas
enflame
envious
fault
firebrands
grievous
hath
heirs
honourable
interred
judgement
mantle
mischief
mourned
muffling
mutiny
offended
orator
overshot
parchment
ransoms
rent
reverence
ruffle
slew
sterner
testament
traitors
triumph
tyrant
valour
vile
withholds

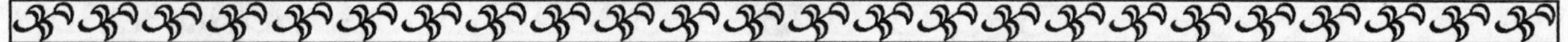

Characters

Soothsayer
Julius Caesar, ruler of Rome
Brutus, Caesar's best friend, a Roman Senator, and a conspirator
Mark Antony, Caesar's second best friend and a Roman officer
Cassius, Roman Senator and conspirator
Casca, Roman Senator and conspirator
Portia, Wife of Brutus
Calpurnia, Wife of Caesar
Servant of Antony
Soldiers
Roman Citizens

Julius Caesar

Scene 1: A Street in Rome Outside the Senate
(Curtain rises on a crowd of citizens as a soldier approaches.)

Soldier: Get ye off the streets. This is a day in honour of Caesar. Clear the streets, for Caesar comes soon.

(People leave. Caesar, Brutus, Cassius, Casca, Antony, and soldiers enter.)

Soothsayer: Beware the Ides of March!

Caesar: What man is that?

Brutus: A soothsayer bids you beware the Ides of March.

Caesar: Set him before me. Let me see his face.

Cassius: You there. Come from the throng, look upon Caesar.

Caesar: What sayest thou to me now? Speak once again.

Soothsayer: Beware the Ides of March.

Caesar: He is a dreamer, let us leave him.

(Caesar and his following enter the senate chamber offstage. Cassius stops Brutus.)

Cassius: Brutus, a word with you. Brutus, I have been watching you lately, and I have not from you that friendliness that I would like to have.

Brutus: Cassius be not fooled. I have had many problems and therefore have neglected my friends.

Cassius: But tell me, good Brutus, can you see your face?

Brutus: No, Cassius, for the eye sees not itself.

Cassius: Many of the best men in Rome have wished that Brutus would use his eyes!

Brutus: Into what dangers are you trying to lead me, Cassius?

Cassius: Good Brutus, be prepared to hear. Since you do not use your eyes to see what is happening to Rome, I will serve as your eyes. Listen to what I have to say!

(A shout is heard from the senate.)

Brutus: What means this shouting? I do fear the people choose Caesar for their king!

Cassius: Aye, do you fear it? Then I must think you would not have it so.

Brutus: I do not like the idea of Caesar being king, yet I do love Caesar well. But Cassius, why do you hold me here so long? What is it you wish to tell me?

Cassius: I was born free as Caesar and so were you! We both have fed as well, and we both can endure the winter's cold as well as he. For once, upon a raw and windy day, standing near the Tiber, Caesar said to me, "Dare you, Cassius, nowleap with me into this angry flood and swim across to the other shore?" Upon this word I plunged in and told him to follow. So he did, but before we could get to the other side, Caesar cried, "Help me Cassius, or I sink!" I then rescued the great mighty Caesar to the shore. This man is now become a god, and Cassius is a wretched creature and must bend his body to Caesar.

(Another shout is heard from the senate.)

Brutus: Another general shout? I do believe that these applauses are for some new honours that are heaped on Caesar.

Cassius: He stands above the narrow world like a Colossus, and we petty men walk under his huge legs and peep about. Brutus and Caesar . . . Why should Caesar's name be sounded more than yours? Write them together and yours is as good a name! Weigh them and they are as heavy! Upon what meat does this our Caesar feed that he has grown so great? I have heard our fathers say that there was once a Brutus that would have attacked the devil himself to save Rome from ruin.

(A third shout is heard from the senate.)

Brutus: What you have said, I will think about. What you have to say, I will with patience listen and find a time to give you an answer. Till then, my noble friend, chew upon this: Brutus would rather be a villager than say he were not a true son of Rome!

Cassius: I'm glad that my weak words have struck a show of fire from Brutus.

Brutus: Caesar is returning!

Cassius: As they pass us, pluck Casca by the sleeve and he will tell us what all the shouting was about.

(Caesar, Antony, Casca, and crowd enter.)

Caesar: Antony!

Antony: Yes, Caesar!

Caesar: Let me have men about me that are fat, and men that sleep at night. Yon Cassius has a lean and hungry look. He thinks too much. Such men are dangerous!

Antony: Fear him not, Caesar, he's not dangerous. He is a noble Roman and well spoken of!

Caesar: I wish that he were fatter, but I fear him not! Yet, if I were afraid, the man I would most avoid would be Cassius. He reads much, he loves not plays, he hears not music, and seldom he smiles. Such men as he are never contented. They are dangerous! I rather tell thee what is to be feared, than what I do fear, for always I am Caesar!

(Caesar and the crowd exit.)

Casca: (To Brutus and Cassius.)
You pulled me by the cloak. What would you speak with me?

Brutus: Tell us what the shouting was about.

Casca: Why, you were with Caesar, were you not?

Brutus: If I had been with him, I would not ask you this question.

Casca: Why, there was a crown offered him, and he pushed it away with the back of his hand, thus. Three times he was offered the crown, and three times he pushed it back. Each time he refused the crown, the people shouted begging him to take the crown.

Cassius: Who offered him the crown?

Casca: Why Antony did.

Cassius: Meet me tonight and we will sup together. Farewell!

(Casca leaves.)

Brutus: At this time I will leave you. If you wish to speak to me further, come to my home.

Cassius: I will do so. Till then, think on Rome! (Brutus leaves.) Well, Brutus, you are noble, yet even you can be influenced to change your mind. Let Caesar seat himself surely, for we will surely shake him!

Scene 2: Late That Night Outside Brutus' House
(Casca and Cassius meet to plot evil. A storm is brewing.)

Casca: It is Caesar that you mean to kill, is it not true, Cassius?

Cassius: Let it be who it is.

Casca: They say the senators tomorrow mean to establish Caesar as a king and he shall wear his crown by sea and land.

Cassius: I know where I will wear this dagger then. Cassius from slavery will deliver Cassius.

Casca: So will I deliver Casca.

Cassius: I have already convinced some of the noblest Romans to join me in my plan. Stand close awhile, for here comes someone in haste.

(They crouch in the darkness until the person has passed.)

Casca: O Cassius, if you could but win the noble Brutus to our side.

Cassius: Do not upset yourself, dear Casca. Take this letter and throw it through Brutus' window, and then meet me at his home.

(Cassius exits. Casca follows instructions, throws the rock, and leaves. Brutus hears the crash and enters.)

Brutus: (Opens the letter and reads.)
"Brutus, you are asleep; awake and see yourself! Shall Rome be under one man's rule?" Since Cassius did speak to me about Caesar, I have not been able to sleep. It has been like a horrible dream making up my mind. (A knock on the door.) Enter!

(Cassius and Casca enter.)

Cassius: Do we trouble you, Brutus?

Brutus: No, I was awake.

Cassius: Every nobleman in Rome waits for your decision.

Brutus: Give me your hands. I am with you!

Cassius: And now let us swear our resolution.

Brutus: No, not an oath, but only to be sure in our hearts that we are doing the right thing.

Casca: Is anyone else to be touched but Caesar?

Cassius: I do not think that Mark Antony would outlive Caesar. Let Antony and Caesar fall together!

Brutus: Let us be sacrificers and not butchers. Let us kill Caesar boldly, but not wrathfully. Let us do all this so that in our hearts we are purgers and not murderers. And as for Mark Antony, think not on him, for he can do no more when Caesar is gone.

Cassius: Yet, I fear him!

Brutus: Alas, good Cassius, do not think of him. If he truly loves Caesar, all that he can do is to die for Caesar!

(Clock strikes three.)

Casca: 'Tis late . . . 'tis time to part.

Cassius: But will Caesar come forth today? He is superstitious grown of late. It may be that the terror of this night and the persuasion of his priests may hold him from the capitol today.

Casca: Never fear. I can oversway him. Let me flatter him. I will bring him to the capitol.

Cassius: The morning comes upon us. We will leave you Brutus. But remember what you have said, and show yourselves true Romans.

(They all leave except Brutus. Portia enters.)

Portia: Brutus, my lord.

Brutus: Portia, my wife. Why do you rise so early? It is not good for you.

Portia: Not for you, either. You stole from your bed this evening, and last night at supper you suddenly arose and walked about thinking and sighing. This thing that bothers you will not let you eat or drink. Brutus, my lord, tell me what is causing you such grief!

Brutus: I am not well in health, and that is all.

Portia: Brutus is wise and, if he were sick, he would do some thing about it.

Brutus: That is what I plan to do. Now go to bed, Portia.

Portia: No, Brutus, you are not physically sick, but you are sick in your mind. Some men came to visit you with their faces hidden. Who were they?

Brutus: Kneel not, gentle Portia.

Portia: I should not have to kneel if you were gentle, Brutus. As your wife, I should know your secret. I am trustworthy, dear Brutus!

Brutus: Oh, ye gods, make me worthy of noble Portia!

Scene 3: Caesar's House the Next Morning

Caesar: Nor heaven, nor earth, have been at peace tonight. Three times hath Calpurnia in her sleep cried out, "Help, ho! They murder Caesar!" Who goes there?

Calpurnia: What mean you, Caesar? You shall not stir out of this house today.

Caesar: Caesar shall go forth!

Calpurnia: Caesar, I am frightened! A lioness hath walked the streets, graves have yawned and yielded up their dead. Fierce, fiery warriors fought upon clouds. The noise of battle hurtled in the air. Horses did neigh, dying men did groan and spirits did shriek and squeal about the streets. O Caesar, these things are beyond all of us, and I do fear them!

Caesar: Yet Caesar shall go forth! Cowards die many times before their deaths. The valiant never taste of death but once!

Calpurnia: Alas, my lord, you are very wise, but do not go out today. Call it *my* fear that keeps you in the house, and not your own. We will send Mark Antony to the senate house, and he shall say you are not well today. Upon my knee, I beg you!

Caesar: Very well. Mark Antony shall say I am not well, and to please you I will stay at home.

(Enter Casca.)

Casca: Hail, O Caesar! I come to take you to the senate house.

Caesar: And you come at a very good time to deliver a message to the senators saying that I will not come today.

Calpurnia: Say he is sick.

Caesar: Shall Caesar send a lie? No! Tell them Caesar will not come!

Casca: Most mighty Caesar, let me know some cause lest they laugh at me when I tell them.

Caesar: I will not come, that is enough to satisfy the senate. But for your private satisfaction, and because you are my friend, I will let *you* know. Calpurnia here, my wife, keeps me at home because she dreamt that she saw my statue surrounded by danger and doom. And for this, she begs I stay home today.

Casca: This dream is all misinterpreted. It was a vision fair and fortunate. The statue signifies that from you great Rome shall be revived. This is what Calpurnia's dream signifies!

Caesar: And this way have you well explained it.

Casca: And know it now, the senate has concluded to give this day a crown to mighty Caesar. If you shall send them word you will not come, their minds may change. You are apt to be mocked when they say, "Break up the senate till another day when Caesar's wife shall meet with better dreams!" If Caesar hide himself, shall they not whisper, "Lo! Caesar is afraid?" Pardon me, Caesar, but my dear, dear love bids me tell you this.

Caesar: How foolish do your fears seem now, Calpurnia! I am ashamed I did yield to them. Give me my robe, for I will go!

Scene 4: The Senate Later in the Morning
(Caesar enters with crowd following.)

Caesar: (To Soothsayer.)
You there. The Ides of March are come!

Soothsayer: Ay, Caesar, but not gone!

(Enter Cassius, Brutus, Casca, and other conspirators.)

Brutus: (Kneeling before Caesar.)
I kiss thy hand!

Cassius: I kneel before thee, O mighty Caesar!

Casca: Speak hands for me!

(Casca stabs Caesar. Cassius stabs Caesar. Brutus stabs Caesar.)

Caesar: Et tu Brute? Then fall, Caesar!

(Caesar dies.)

Brutus: People, be not afraid. Ambition's debt is paid!

Casca: Liberty . . . Freedom . . . Tyranny are dead! Yell it about the streets!

(The crowd leaves.)

Cassius: Where is Mark Antony?

Casca: He has fled to his house amazed!

(Servant enters.)

Brutus: Who comes here?

Servant: My master, Mark Antony, bid me come and say that Brutus is noble, wise, brave, and honest. Mark Antony asks if he might visit Caesar's body without any harm coming to him.

Brutus: Thy master, Mark Antony, is a wise and valiant Roman. Tell him he shall be satisfied and, by my honour, depart untouched.

Servant: I'll fetch him presently.

(Servant exits.)

Brutus: I know we shall have Mark Antony as a friend.

Cassius: I wish we may! But yet, I have misgivings. I fear him much!

Brutus: But here comes Antony. (Antony enters.) Welcome, Mark Antony!

Antony: O mighty Caesar! Do you lie so low? Are all your conquests and glories fallen to this? Fare thee well! If I live a thousand years, I shall find no better place to die than right here next to Caesar!

Brutus: O Antony, beg not your death from us. Though now we must appear cruel, you see but our hands and this the business they have done. You do not see our hearts!

Cassius: Your voice shall be as strong as any man's in the new government.

Brutus: Only be patient till we have appeased the multitude, and then we will explain to you the cause, why I, that did love Caesar, did strike him.

Antony: I doubt not your wisdom. Let each man give me his hand. All I ask is that I may take his body to the market place and speak to the public at his funeral.

Brutus: You shall, Mark Antony.

Cassius: Brutus, a word with you! (Aside to Brutus.) You know not what you do! Do not consent that Antony speak at Caesar's funeral. Know you not how much people may be moved by that which he will utter?

Brutus: (Aside to Cassius.)
By your pardon, I will myself into the pulpit first, and show the reason of our Caesar's death. What Antony shall speak, I will say he speaks by our leave and our permission.

Cassius: (Aside to Brutus.)
I know not what may fall. I like it not!

Brutus: Mark Antony, here take you Caesar's body. You shall not in your funeral speech blame us, but speak all good you can devise of Caesar. Say you do it by our permission, or else you shall not have any hand at all about his funeral. And you shall speak in the same pulpit whereto I am going, after my speech is ended.

Antony: Be it so. I do desire no more.

Brutus: Prepare the body then, and follow us.

(All exit but Antony.)

Antony: (Kneeling beside Caesar's body.)
O pardon me, that I am meek and gentle with these cruel men. Thou art the ruins of the noblest man that ever lived in the tide of times. Woe to the hands that shed this costly blood! Over thy wounds, now I do prophesy. A curse shall fall on those who have done this deed!

(Soldier enters and helps Antony carry Caesar off stage.)

Scene 5: The Roman Forum That Afternoon
(Brutus is standing before the crowd of Roman citizens.)

Citizens: We will be satisfied! Let us be satisfied!

Brutus: Then follow me, and give me audience, friends.

First Citizen: I will hear Brutus speak!

Second Citizen: And I!

(Brutus climbs to pulpit.)

Third Citizen: The noble Brutus is ascended. Silence!

Brutus: Romans, countrymen, and friends hear me for my cause, and be silent that you may hear. If there be any in the assembly, any dear friend of Caesar's, to him I say that Brutus' love to Caesar was no less than his. If then, that friend demand why Brutus rose against Caesar, this is my answer—not that I loved Caesar less, but that I loved Rome more! Had you rather Caesar were living, and die all slaves, than that Caesar were dead, to live all free men? As Caesar loved me, I weep for him; as he was valiant, I honour him; but as he was ambitious, I slew him! There are tears for his love, honour for his valour, and death for his ambition! Who is here so base that would be a slave! If any, speak, for him have I offended. Who is here so rude that would not be a Roman? If any, speak, for him have I offended. Who is here so vile that will not love his country? If any, speak, for him have I offended!

Citizens: None, Brutus, none!

Brutus: Then none have I offended! (Enter Antony and soldier with Caesar's body.) Here comes his body, mourned by Mark Antony, who though he had no hand in Caesar's death, shall receive the benefit of Caesar's dying, as which of you shall not? With this I depart, that as I slew my best friend for the good of Rome, I have the same dagger for myself, when it shall please my country to need my death!

Citizens: Live, Brutus, live!

Fourth Citizen: Bring him with triumph home unto his house!

Fifth Citizen: Give him a statue with his ancestors!

Sixth Citizen: Let him be Caesar!

Brutus: My countrymen . . .

Seventh Citizen: Peace! Silence! Brutus speaks! . . . Peace!

Brutus: Good countrymen, let me depart alone. And for my sake, stay here with Antony. Do grace to Caesar's body, and grace his speech tending to Caesar's glories, which Mark

Antony by our permission is allowed to make. I do entreat you, not a man depart, save I alone, till Antony has spoken.

(Brutus exits.)

Eighth Citizen: Stay ho! And let us hear Mark Antony!

Ninth Citizen: Let him go up to the pulpit. We will hear him! Noble Antony go up!

Antony: For Brutus' sake, I am beholden to you.

(Climbs to pulpit.)

Tenth Citizen: This Caesar was a tyrant!

First Citizen: Speak no harm of Brutus here!

Second Citizen: Rome is blessed to be rid of Caesar!

Third Citizen: Peace! Let us hear what Antony can say.

Antony: You gentle Romans . . .

Fourth Citizen: Peace ho! Let us hear him!

Antony: Friends, Romans, countrymen, lend me your ears! I come to bury Caesar, not to praise him. The evil that men do lives after them. The good is oft interred with their bones. So let is be with Caesar. The noble Brutus hath told you Caesar was ambitious. If it were so, it was a grievous fault, and grievously hath Caesar paid for it. Here, under leave of Brutus and the rest, for Brutus is an honourable man, so are they all honourable men. I come to speak at Caesar's funeral. He was my friend, faithful and just to me but Brutus says he was ambitious and Brutus is an honourable man. He hath brought many captives home to Rome, whose ransoms did the general coffers fill. Did this in Caesar seem ambitious? When that the poor had cried, Caesar hath wept! Ambition should be made of sterner stuff; yet Brutus says he was ambitious, and Brutus is an honourable man. You all do remember that I three times presented him with a kingly crown, which he did three times refuse! Was this ambition? Yet Brutus says he was ambitious, and surely Brutus is an honourable man! I speak not to disprove what Brutus spoke, but here I am to speak what I do know. You all did love him once, not without cause! What cause withholds you then to mourn for him? O judgement, thou are fled to brutish beasts, and men have lost their reason. Bear with me, my heart is in the coffin there with Caesar, and I must pause till it come back to me.

Fifth Citizen: There is much reason in his sayings.

Sixth Citizen: If you consider the matter rightly, Caesar has had great wrong!

Seventh Citizen: Caesar did not take the crown; therefore he was not ambitious!

Eighth Citizen: There's not a nobler man in Rome than Antony!

Ninth Citizen: Listen! He begins to speak again!

Antony: But yesterday, the word of Caesar might have stood against the world. Now he lies there, with no one to do him reverence. But here is a parchment with the seal of Caesar. I found it in his room. It is his will! If the people were to hear this testament which, pardon me, I do not mean to read, they would go and kiss Caesar's wounds!

Tenth Citizen: We will hear the will. Read it, Mark Antony!

Citizens: The will! The will! We will hear Caesar's will!

Antony: Have patience, gentle friends, I must not read it. It is not proper that you should know how much Caesar loved you. You are not wood, you are not stones, but men! And being men, hearing the will of Caesar, it will enflame you and it will make you mad. It is good that you know not that you are his heirs, for if you should, O what would come of it?

First Citizen: We will hear the will, Antony! You shall read us the will!

Antony: Will you be patient? Will you stay awhile? I have overshot myself to tell you of it. I fear I wrong the honourable men whose daggers have stabbed Caesar. I do fear it!

Second Citizen: Honourable men? They were traitors!

Citizens: The will! The testament!

Third Citizen: They were villains! Read the will!

Antony: You will compel me then to read the will?

Citizens:	The will! The will! The will! The will!
Antony:	Then let me show you him that made the will. (Descends from pulpit and stands by Caesar's body.) If you have tears, prepare to shed them now. You all do know this mantle. I remember the first time ever Caesar put it on. Look, in this place ran Cassius' dagger through. See what a rent the envious Casca made! Through this, the well-beloved Brutus stabbed! Judge, O you gods, how Caesar loved him. This was the unkindest cut of all! For when the noble Caesar saw him stab, then burst his mighty heart. His mantle muffling up his face at the base of Pompey's statue great Caesar fell! O what a fall was there my countrymen! O now you weep!
Fourth Citizen:	O noble Caesar!
Fifth Citizen:	O woeful day!
Sixth Citizen:	Traitors . . . Villains! We will be revenged!
Citizens:	Revenge! Let not a traitor live!
Antony:	Stay, countrymen.
Seventh Citizen:	Peace! Hear the noble Antony!
Eighth Citizen:	We'll hear him! We'll follow him! We'll die with him!
Antony:	Good friends, sweet friends, let me not stir you up to a sudden mutiny. They that have done this deed are honourable. Alas, I know not what made them do it. They are wise and honourable and will no doubt tell you their reasons. I come not, friends, to steal away your hearts. I am no orator as Brutus is, but as you know me all, a plain, blunt man that loved my friend. For I have neither wit nor words, nor the power of speech, to stir men's blood. I only show you Caesar's wounds, poor, poor dumb mouths, and bid them speak to me. *But* were I Brutus, and Brutus Antony, I would ruffle up your spirits and put a tongue in every wound of Caesar that would move the stones of Rome to rise and mutiny!
Citizens:	We will mutiny!
Ninth Citizen:	We'll burn the house of Brutus!
Antony:	Yet hear me speak, countrymen, yet hear me speak.

Tenth Citizen:	Hear most noble Antony. Hear him!
Antony:	Why, friends, you go to do you know not what. You have forgot the will I told of.
Citizens:	The will! The will! The will! Let's hear the will!
Antony:	Here is the will, and under Caesar's seal! To every Roman he gives seventy-five drachmas!
First Citizen:	Most noble Caesar! We'll revenge his death!
Second Citizen:	O royal Caesar!
Antony:	Hear me with patience! Moreover, he hath left you all his walks, his private arbours, and new planted orchards. Here was a Caesar! When comes such another?
Third Citizen:	Never! Never!
Fourth Citizen:	We'll burn his body in the holy place, and with the firebrands we will burn the houses of the traitors!
Fifth Citizen:	Take up the body!
Sixth Citizen:	Go fetch fire!
Citizens:	Fire!
	(Citizens leave with the body of Caesar.)
Antony:	Now let it work. Mischief, thou art afoot. Take thou what course thou wilt!

The Comedy of Errors

Introduction

The Comedy of Errors is a fast-moving comedy based on misunderstandings that a double pair of twins can present. The most important idea to implant in the cast and the audience is that the stage represents the city of Ephesus and the people entering through another door, from the back of the auditorium, or from a side aisle are people from the city of Syracuse. "S" stands for strangers from Syracuse, and once this fact is established, there are no identity problems.

Twins, of course, are not needed to play the twin parts in the play. Simply have the two Antipholuses wear the same style wig. The two Dromios can wear bald skin caps.

Characterization in this play should be very exaggerated. The Duke should be aristocratic to the hilt. Old Aegeon should be pathetically helpless and the merchants should speak clearly and pompously.

All during the performance, your audience will laugh so much that the actors will have to hold their characterizations to be understood.

Staging

Scene 1
On a full stage, the citizens of Ephesus gather around their Duke to hear the sad, sad tale of old Aegeon, which causes the crowd to cry obvious tears.

Scene 2
This scene should be staged in front of the curtain, which is designated as the interior of the house of Antipholus of Ephesus.

Scene 3
The curtain opens to reveal the market place.

Scene 4
This scene is staged in front of the curtain, which this time is designated as the outside of the house of Antipholus. A plain door held in place by two servants as

Antipholus of Ephesus pounds on it will create an outside mood.

Scene 5
The door is removed, and again the area in front of the curtain becomes the interior of Antipholus' house.

Scenes 6-7
The curtain opens to the market place again.

Scene 8
Use the full stage to enact this most comedic attempt to tie up Antipholus of Ephesus and Dromio of Ephesus.

Scene 9
Position two poles with a piece of cloth attached between them to represent the entrance to the abbey.

Costumes

Costumes can be simple. Dress the sets of twins in tunics. Old Aegeon can wear rags and the Duke and merchants can wear long robes.

Vocabulary

Scene 1
approach
attend
brief
capon
comical
commend
content
deceive
deform
disguised
doom
encountered
fastened
gaze
hapless
inquisitive
jests
jugglers
knave
marks
mast
nimble
peasant
pity
plead
proceed
profusely
prosperous
ransom
sixpence
sorcerer
sought
trickery
woes

Scene 2	fetch	haste
dine	fond	hither
doubtfully	fret	spurn

Scene 3	fasten	spite
ay	fie	sprites
converse	heedful	transformed
dame	inspiration	vein
drone	pate	villain
elm	porter	yonder
ensue	snail	

Scene 4	linger	signor
depart	prevailed	unruly
disdain		

Scene 5	doomsday	trudge
abhor	inhabit	wench
comfort	shifts	

Scene 6	debt	persuasion
bail	fee	purse
consent	fulfill	reputation
consider	goldsmith	statement
debate	leisure	tempt

Scene 7	ducats	sorceress
acquainted	salute	

Scene 8	frantic	wan
conjurer	pluck	wizard
fiend	possession	yield
fiery	Satan	

Scene 9	execution	positive
abbess	fled	priory
abbey	gracious	proclaim
accidentally	grievous	publicly
acknowledge	hindered	renown
bind	misery	sanctuary
distracted	originally	verify
embrace	outrageous	wits

Characters

Duke of Ephesus
Aegeon, merchant of Syracuse
Antipholus of Ephesus
Dromio of Ephesus, servant of Antipholus of Ephesus
Antipholus of Syracuse
Dromio of Syracuse, servant of Antipholus of Syracuse
Balthazar, merchant of Ephesus
Angelo, goldsmith
Aemilia, abbess of Ephesus
Adriana, wife of Antipholus of Ephesus
Luciana, Adriana's sister
Luce, servant of Adriana
Merchant
Doctor Pinch
Officer
Woman
Citizens of Ephesus

The Comedy of Errors

Scene 1: The Market Place in Ephesus in the Morning
(Citizens and officers are gathered around Aegeon and their Duke.)

Aegeon: Proceed to bring about my fall, and by the doom of death end woes and all.

Duke: Merchant of Syracuse, plead no more, for it is useless. Both the laws of Syracuse and our laws of Ephesus state that any born at Ephesus cannot be seen at Syracusian markets, and if any Syracusian born come to the bay of Ephesus . . . he dies unless a thousand golden coins be paid for his ransom. If you cannot produce the thousand coins, by law thou art condemned to die!

Aegeon: My only comfort, when your words are done, my woes end likewise with the evening sun.

Duke: Well, Syracusian, say in brief the cause why you left your native home of Syracuse, and what cause brought you to our Ephesus.

Aegeon: In Syracuse was I born and wed unto a woman where we lived in joy. Our wealth increased. Many prosperous voyages I often made to Epidamnum and my wife joined me. While there she became a joyful mother of twin boys. That very hour, in the self-same inn, a peasant woman also gave birth to male twins, both alike. Since they were very poor, I bought the peasant twins to attend my twin sons. Upon our return home we sailed into a storm. The sailors sought for safety and left the ship. My wife fastened one twin and a servant twin unto a mast, and I did the same with the other two. When the sets of twins were cared for, my wife and I also fastened ourselves to masts. Lo and behold, two ships from afar off were making toward us . . . but oh! Let me say no more!

(Begins comical sobbing.)

Duke: Do not stop so! For we may pity, though not pardon thee.

Aegeon: Before the ships could reach us, we were encountered by a mighty rock. Our helpful ship was split in two! One ship gathered up my wife and two children, while I was saved with the other set of twins by the other ship.

(More comical sobbing.)

Duke: Tell us what happened to them and thee!

Aegeon: My youngest boy at eighteen years became inquisitive about his brother and asked to search for him with his servant twin. Five summers now have I searched for my sons. Five summers have I spent in Greece, roaming clear through the bounds of Asia, and coasting homeward come to Ephesus. But here must end the story of my life!

(More sobbing.)

Duke: Hapless Aegeon! Even though the laws of Ephesus say death to thee, I'll give thee a day to save thy life. Try all the friends thou hast in Ephesus to raise the thousand golden coins that will save thy life. Beg or borrow to make up the sum, and live. If no, then thou art doomed to die. Officer, take him away!

Officer: I will, my lord.

(As the officer drags off old Aegeon, the Duke of Ephesus and the citizens of Ephesus cry profusely in their silken handkerchiefs. The stage empties as the crowd follows the jailer. Enter Antipholus of Syracuse and a merchant.)

Merchant: Tell no one you are from Syracuse. There is your money that I had to keep!

Antipholus of Syracuse: Go, Dromio, and give it to the innkeeper where we stay, and stay there, Dromio, till I come to thee. Within this hour it will be dinner time. Till then I'll view the manners of the town, gaze upon the buildings, and then return and sleep at the inn. With long travel I am stiff and weary. Get thee away.

Dromio of Syracuse: Yes, my lord.

(Exits.)

Antipholus of Syracuse: Will you walk with me about the town and then go to my inn and dine with me?

Merchant: I have already been invited. My present business calls me from you now. I'll meet you here at the marketplace at five o'clock.

Antipholus of Syracuse: Farewell till then. I will go lose myself and wander up and down to view the city.

Merchant: Sir, I commend you to your own content.

(Exits.)

Antipholus of Syracuse: (Speaking to audience.)
He that commends me to mine own content, commends me to the thing I cannot get. I, to the world am like a drop of water, that in the ocean seeks another drop. I seek to find a mother and a brother . . . in quest of them, unhappy, lose myself. (Enter Dromio of Ephesus.) What now? How come you have returned so soon!

Dromio of Ephesus: Returned so soon? Rather approached too late! The capon burns, the pig galls from the spit, the clock hath struck twelve upon the bell, my mistress made it one upon my cheek. She is angry because the meat is cold, the meat is cold because you come not home!

Antipholus of Syracuse: Stop! Now, tell me, where have you left the money that I gave you?

Dromio of Ephesus: O, the sixpence that I had on Wednesday last to pay to have the saddle repaired for your mistress? I kept it not.

Antipholus of Syracuse: I am not in a joking mood. Tell me and dally not, where is the gold?

Dromio of Ephesus: The gold? You gave no gold to me!

Antipholus of Syracuse: Come, Dromio, these jests are out of season. Save them for a merrier hour than this. Where is the gold I gave in charge to thee?

Dromio of Ephesus: To me, sir? Why, you gave no gold to me!

Antipholus of Syracuse: Come, knave have done with your foolishness and tell me how you did your errand.

Dromio of Ephesus: My errand was but to get you from the market place home to your house to dinner. Your wife and her sister await you.

Antipholus of Syracuse: Now, you listen here, you answer me! In what safe place have you placed my money, or I shall break that merry head of yours? Where are the thousand marks I gave you?

Dromio of Ephesus: I have some marks of yours upon my head, some of my mistress' marks upon my shoulder, but not a thousand marks between you both.

Antipholus of Syracuse: Thy mistress' marks? What mistress slave hast thou?

Dromio of Ephesus: *Your* wife, my mistress. She that waits till you come home to dinner, and prays that you will hurry.

Antipholus of Syracuse: What? Will you make fun of me right before my face? . . . There . . . take that!

(Strikes him.)

Dromio of Ephesus: What mean you, sir? For God's sake, hold your hands!

(Exits in confusion.)

Antipholus of Syracuse: They say this town is full of trickery, as nimble jugglers that deceive the eye, disguised cheaters, and many such evil people. I will go to the inn to seek that slave. I greatly fear my money is not safe!

Scene 2: Early Afternoon Inside the House of Antipholus of Ephesus
(Adriana and her sister are chatting.)

Adriana: Neither my husband nor the slave that in such haste I sent to see his master have returned. It must be two o'clock, Luciana.

Luciana: Perhaps some merchant hath invited him and from the market he has gone somewhere to dinner. Good sister, let us dine and never fret. A man is master of his liberty. Here comes your servant now.

(Enter Dromio of Ephesus.)

Adriana: Say, is your tardy master now at hand?

Dromio of Ephesus: Nay, he's at two hands with me, and that, my two ears can witness.

Adriana: Say, did you speak with him? Do you know his mind?

Dromio of Ephesus: Ay, he told his mind upon mine ear.

Luciana: Did he speak so doubtfully that you could not understand his meaning?

Dromio of Ephesus: O, I understood his meaning!

(He rubs his aching head.)

Adriana: But, I say, is he coming home?

Dromio of Ephesus: When I asked him to come home to dinner, he asked me for a thousand marks in gold.
"Tis dinner time," said I.
"My gold," said he.
"Your meat doth burn," said I.
"My gold," said he.
"Will you come home?" said I.
"My gold," said he.
"The pig is burned," said I.
"My gold," said he.
"My mistress, sir," said I.
"I know not your mistress . . . I know no house or wife."
And then he did beat me here and here!

(He begins to howl.)

Adriana: Go back again, thou slave, and fetch him home.

Dromio of Ephesus: Go back again, and be beaten again?

Adriana: Back slave, or I will break thy head. Fetch thy master home!

Dromio of Ephesus: Am I so round with you as you with me, that like a ball you do spurn me thus? You spurn me hence, and he will spurn me hither. If I last in this service, you must case me in leather. (Exits.)

Adriana: My beauty doth fade, and his eyes look toward others or else he would be here. Sister, you know he promised me a chain. Since my beauty can no longer please his eyes. I'll weep what's left away and weeping die.

(Exits crying wildly.)

Luciana: How many fond fools serve mad jealousy!

Scene 3: The Market Place Half an Hour Later

Antipholus of Syracuse: The gold I gave to Dromio is safe at the inn and heedful slave is wandered off to seek me out. See, here he comes. (Enter Dromio of Syracuse.) And now sir, has your mad humor changed? Will you jest with me again? You received no gold? Your mistress sent you to have me home to dinner? Wast thou mad?

Dromio of Syracuse: When did I speak such words?

Antipholus of Syracuse: Not half an hour ago!

Dromio of Syracuse: I did not see you since you sent me to the inn with the gold.

Antipholus of Syracuse: Villain! You denied having the gold and you told me of a mistress and a dinner.

Dromio of Syracuse: I am glad to see you in this merry vein. What means this jest? I pray you master, tell me.

Antipholus of Syracuse: Dost thou make fun of me and think that I jest? Take that and that!

(He strikes Dromio.)

Dromio of Syracuse: Enough, sir! Hold! I pray, sir, why am I beaten?

Antipholus of Syracuse: Does thou not know?

Dromio of Syracuse: Nothing, sir, but that I am beaten.

Antipholus of Syracuse: Shall I tell you why?

Dromio of Syracuse: Ay sir.

Antipholus of Syracuse: First, for making fun of me, and then for making fun the second time!

Dromio of Syracuse: Was there ever a man thus beaten out of season, when in the why and wherefore is neither rhyme nor reason? Well, sir, I thank you.

Antipholus of Syracuse: Thank me! For what?

Dromio of Syracuse: For this something you gave me for nothing!

Antipholus of Syracuse: But soft, who comes yonder?

(Enter Adriana and Luciana.)

Adriana: Antipholus, I am Adriana, thy wife. O how comes it, husband, that thou art thus so strange?

Antipholus of Syracuse: Plead you to me, fair dame? I know you not! In Ephesus I am but two hours old, as strange unto your town as to your talk.

Luciana: Fie brother, how the world is changed with you! Why do you treat my sister thus? She sent for you by Dromio home to dinner.

Antipholus of Syracuse: By Dromio?

Dromio of Syracuse: By me?

Adriana: By thee! Did you not return from him saying that he did strike you and denied having a house and a wife?

Antipholus of Syracuse: Did you converse with this gentle woman?

Dromio of Syracuse: I, sir? Never saw her till this time!

Antipholus of Syracuse: How can she thus call us by our names unless it be by inspiration?

Adriana: Come! I will fasten on this sleeve of thine. Thou art an elm, my husband, and I a vine.

Antipholus of Syracuse: To me she speaks! What? Was I married to her in my dream? Or sleep I now, and think I hear all this?

Luciana: Dromio, go bid the servant spread for dinner.

Dromio of Syracuse: This is a fairyland. O spite of spites! We talk with goblins, owls, and elvish sprites. If we obey them not, this will ensue . . . they'll suck our breath or pinch us black and blue!

Luciana: What? Talkest to thy self? Dromio, thou drone, thou snail!

Dromio of Syracuse: I am transformed, master, am not I?

Antipholus of Syracuse: I think thou art, and so am I!

Adriana: Come, no longer will I be a fool to put the finger in the eye and weep. Come, husband, to dinner. Come, sister. Dromio, take care of the gate and play the porter well.

Antipholus of Syracuse: (Aside.)

Am I in earth, in heaven, or hell? Sleeping or walking?

Dromio of Syracuse: Master, shall I be porter at the gate?

Adriana: Ay, and let none enter lest I break your pate!

Luciana: Come, Antipholus, we dine too late!

Scene 4: A Little Later in Front of the House of Antipholus of Ephesus
(Enter Antipholus of Ephesus, Angelo, and Balthazar.)

Antipholus of Ephesus: Good Signor Angelo, you must excuse us all. My wife is shrewish when I keep her waiting. I'll say that I lingered with you at your shop to see the making of her golden chain and that tomorrow you will bring it home. (Enter

Dromio of Ephesus.) But here's the villain that said I did deny my wife and house. What did you mean by this?

Dromio of Ephesus: Say what you will, sir, but I know what I know, that you beat me at the market place. I have your hand to show!

Antipholus of Ephesus: I think thou art a fool. But soft, my door is locked! Go bid them let me in.

Dromio of Ephesus: Maud, Bridget, Marian . . .

Dromio of Syracuse: (From within.)

Go. Get thee from the door!

Dromio of Ephesus: My master is waiting in the street!

Dromio of Syracuse: (From within.)
Let him walk!

Antipholus of Ephesus: Who talks within there? Open the door! What art thou that keepest me out from mine own house?

Dromio of Syracuse: (From within.)
The porter, sir, and my name is Dromio!

Dromio of Ephesus: O villain! Thou hast stolen both mine office and my name!

Adriana: (From within.)
Who is that at the door that makes all this noise?

Dromio of Syracuse: (From within.)
The town is troubled with unruly boys.

Antipholus of Ephesus: Are you there, wife? You might have come before!

Adriana: (From within.)
Your wife, sir? You knave! Go! Get you from the door!

Antipholus of Ephesus: Go? Get thee gone? Fetch me an iron bar!

Balthazar: Have patience, sir. Let it not be so. Let not yourself be caught in such an embarrassing situation, locked out by your wife. Depart in patience, and later in the evening return by yourself.

Antipholus of Ephesus: You have prevailed. I will depart in quiet. However, I mean to be merry. (To Angelo.) Deliver the golden chain to the House of Porpentine. Since mine own doors refuse to entertain me, I'll knock elsewhere to see if they'll disdain me.

Angelo: I'll meet you at that place in an hour or so.

Scene 5: Later Inside the House of Antipholus of Ephesus

Luciana: And may it be you have quite forgot your place as a husband? Gentle brother, get you in. Comfort my sister, cheer her, call her wife.

Antipholus of Syracuse: Sweet mistress, your weeping sister is no wife of mine. Far more, far more to you do I kneel.

Luciana: What! Are you mad, that you do reason so?

Antipholus of Syracuse: It is you I love, and with thee I will lead my life! Thou hast no husband yet, nor I no wife. Give me thy hand.

Luciana: Hold you still! I'll fetch my sister, to get her good will.

(Exit Luciana. Enter Dromio of Syracuse.)

Antipholus of Syracuse: Why, how now, Dromio! Where runnest thou so fast?

Dromio of Syracuse: Do you know me, sir? Am I Dromio? Am I your servant? Am I myself?

Antipholus of Syracuse: You are Dromio, thou art my servant, thou art thyself!

Dromio of Syracuse: I belong to some woman! One that claims me, one that haunts me!

Antipholus of Syracuse: What woman? What claims lays she to thee?

Dromio of Syracuse: She claims she's my wife! She is the kitchen wench and all grease! If she lives till doomsday, she'll burn a week longer than the whole world.

Antipholus of Syracuse: Go! Get thee to the road! And if the wind blow any way from the shore, I will not stay in this town tonight. If any ship comes into port, come to the market where I will walk till you return. If everyone knows us and we know none, 'tis time I think to trudge, pack, and be gone.

Dromio of Syracuse: As from a bear a man would run for life, so fly I from her that would be my wife!

(Exits.)

Antipholus of Syracuse: 'Tis time that I were gone. She that calls me husband, even my soul doth for a wife abhor. Ah, but for her fair sister!

(Enter Angelo with the golden chain.)

Angelo: Master Antipholus?

Antipholus of Syracuse: Ay, That's my name.

Angelo: I know it well, sir. Lo, here is the chain.

Antipholus of Syracuse: What shall I do with it?

Angelo: Why, sir, I have made it for you!

Antipholus of Syracuse: Made it for me, sir? I did not ask for it!

Angelo: Not once, not twice, but twenty times you have! Go home with it, and please your wife, and soon at supper time I'll visit you, and then receive my money for the chain.

Antipholus of Syracuse: I pray you, sir, receive the money now, for fear you'll never see the chain or money again!

Angelo: You are a merry man, sir; fare you well.

(Exits, leaving the chain.)

Antipholus of Syracuse: What I should think of this I cannot tell, but this I think, there's no man so vain that would refuse so fair an offered chain. I see a man here needs not love by shifts, when in the streets he meets such golden gifts. I'll head for the market, and there for Dromio stay; if any ship put, then straight away.

Scene 6: Half-Hour Later in the Market Place of Ephesus
(The Merchant, Angelo, and an Officer are talking.)

Merchant: You know since quite awhile you have owed me money, and now that I am bound on a long journey, I want my money. If I am not satisfied, I will have you arrested by this officer.

Angelo: Just the sum I owe you is owed to me by Antipholus. At five o'clock I will receive the money from him. Will you please walk with me down to his house?

(Enter Antipholus of Ephesus and Dromio of Ephesus.)

Officer: We will be saved the trip. Here he comes now.

Antipholus of Ephesus: While I go to the goldsmith's house, you go buy a rope. But soft, I see the goldsmith. Get thee gone, buy a rope, and bring it home to me. (Exit Dromio of Ephesus. Antipholus turns to Angelo.) You promised to deliver the golden chain, but neither chain nor goldsmith came to me.

Angelo: You are in a merry humour. Here is the statement telling how much your chain weighs and the fineness of the gold. I stand in debt to this gentleman, so I pray you see him presently paid, for he puts out to sea soon and needs the money.

Antipholus of Ephesus: I don't have the money with me, besides, I have some business in town. Good Signor, take the gentleman with you to my house and with you take the chain, and tell my wife to give you the money. I probably will be there when you arrive.

Angelo: Then will you bring the chain to her yourself? Have you the chain about you?

Antipholus of Ephesus: I have not. I hope you have, sir, or else you will return without your money.

Angelo: Come, I pray you, give me the chain.

Merchant: The hour steals on! I pray you, sir, hurry!

Angelo: The chain, sir?

Antipholus of Ephesus:	Why, give it to my wife, and fetch your money.
Angelo:	Come, come! You know I gave it to you.
Antipholus of Ephesus:	Come now, this is no longer funny. Where is the chain? I pray you, let me see it!
Merchant:	My business cannot wait any longer. Good sir, say yes or no, if not, I'll leave him to the officer.
Antipholus of Ephesus:	I answer you! What should I answer you?
Angelo:	The money that you owe me for the chain.
Antipholus of Ephesus:	I owe you none till I receive the chain.
Angelo:	You know I gave it to you half hour ago.
Antipholus of Ephesus:	You gave me none. You wrong me much to say so.
Angelo:	You wrong me more in denying it. Consider how it stands upon my credit.
Merchant:	Well, officer, arrest him!
Officer:	I do, and charge you in the Duke's name to obey me!
Angelo:	This ruins my reputation. Either consent to pay what you owe, or I'll have the officer arrest you!
Antipholus of Ephesus:	Consent to pay thee for what I never had! Arrest me, foolish fellow, if thou darest!
Angelo:	Here is thy fee. Arrest him, officer.
Officer:	I do arrest you, sir!
Antipholus of Ephesus:	I do obey thee until I get bail. But, my dear Angelo, you will regret this very hour.
	(Enter Dromio of Syracuse.)
Dromio of Syracuse:	Master, there is a ship from Epidamnum that is ready to sail. They are waiting for you.
Antipholus of Ephesus:	What? What ship of Epidamnum waits for me?

Dromio of Syracuse:	A ship you sent me to hire.
Antipholus of Syracuse:	I sent thee for a rope! I will debate this matter at more leisure and teach your ears to listen to me. Villain, get thee straight to Adriana. Give her this key and tell her in the desk there is a purse of gold. Tell her I am arrested in the street, and that she should bail me out. Get thee gone, slave!
	(Exit Merchant, Angelo, Officer, and Antipholus of Ephesus.)
Dromio of Syracuse:	To Adriana! This is where we dined . . . where the fat one did claim me for her husband. However, I must go against my will, for servants must their masters' minds fulfill!
	(Exit Dromio of Syracuse. Enter Adriana and Luciana.)
Adriana:	Did he tempt thee so?
Luciana:	First he denied you were his wife, then he swore that he was a stranger here.
Adriana:	With what persuasion did he tempt thy love?
Luciana:	First he did praise my beauty, then my speech. Have patience, I pray you.
	(Enter Dromio of Syracuse.)
Adriana:	Where is thy master, Dromio? Is he well?
Dromio of Syracuse:	No, he is not well!
Adriana:	What is the matter?
Dromio of Syracuse:	He has been arrested!
Adriana:	For what reason?
Dromio of Syracuse:	I do not know the reason, but he bid you get the money in his desk to bail him out.
Adriana:	Go fetch it, sister. (Exit Luciana.) This I wonder at, that he unknown to me should be in debt! (Re-enter Luciana

with the money.) Go, Dromio, there's the money. Bear it straight, and bring thy master home immediately.

Scene 7: Same Place a Half Hour Later
(Antipholus of Syracuse is strolling about alone.)

Antipholus of Syracuse: There's not a man I meet but doth salute me as if I were well acquainted friend; and everyone doth call me by my name. Some give me money, some invite me, others give me thanks for kindnesses. Even now a tailor called me in his shop and showed me silks that he hath bought for me.

(Enter Dromio of Syracuse.)

Dromio of Syracuse: Master, here's the gold you sent me for.

Antipholus of Syracuse: What gold is this? I understand thee not! Now tell me, is any ship sailing forth tonight?

Dromio of Syracuse: Why, sir, I brought you word an hour ago that a ship sails tonight.

Antipholus of Syracuse: You are not well, Nor am I! Some blessed power deliver us from here.

(Enter Woman.)

Woman: Well met, well met, Master Antipholus. I see you found the goldsmith. Is that the chain you promised me today? Remember your promise at supper?

Antipholus of Syracuse: What tellest me of supper? Leave me and be gone!

Woman: Give me the ring of mine you had at dinner or the chain you promised, and I'll be gone, sir, and not trouble you. I hope you do not mean to cheat me?

Antipholus of Syracuse: Away! Come Dromio, let us go!

(Exit Antipholus of Syracuse and Dromio of Syracuse.)

Woman: There is no doubt that Antipholus is mad. A ring he hath of mine that is worth forty ducats, and for the same he promised me a chain. Both one and the other he denies me now. I will rush to his wife and tell her that by force he took my ring away. Forty ducats is too much to lose.

Scene 8: A Street in Ephesus a Few Minutes Later
(Enter Antipholus of Ephesus with the Officer.)

Antipholus of Ephesus: Fear me not, man, I will not break away. (Enter Dromio of Ephesus with a rope.) Here comes my servant. I think he brings the money. How now, have you what I sent you for? Where's the money?

Dromio of Ephesus: Why sir, I gave the money for the rope.

(Antipholus of Ephesus strikes Dromio of Ephesus.)

Officer: Good sir, be patient.

Antipholus of Ephesus: Thou senseless villain!

Dromio of Ephesus: I would I were senseless, sir, that I might not feel your blows!

Antipholus of Ephesus: Come, go along . . . My wife is coming yonder.

(Enter Adriana, Luciana, the Woman and Doctor Pinch.)

Dromio of Ephesus: Mistress, beware!

Antipholus of Ephesus: Wilt thou still talk?

(Antipholus of Ephesus strikes Dromio of Ephesus again.)

Woman: How say you now? Is not your husband mad?

Adriana: Good Doctor Pinch, you are a conjurer. Make him himself again, and I will give you whatever you demand.

Luciana: Alas, how fiery and how sharp he looks!

Pinch: Give me your hand, and let me feel your pulse.

Antipholus of Ephesus: There is my hand, and let it feel your ear.

(He strikes Doctor Pinch.)

Pinch: He is mad!

Antipholus of Ephesus: Thou crazy wizard! I am not mad! Why were the doors of my home shut, and I was not allowed to enter?

Adriana: O husband, why you know you dined at home.

Antipholus of Ephesus: Dined at home! Thou villain, what sayest thou?

Dromio of Ephesus: You did not dine at home.

Antipholus of Ephesus: Were not my doors locked, and I shut out?

Antipholus of Ephesus: Did you convince the goldsmith to arrest me?

Adriana: Alas, I sent you money to bail you out by Dromio here, who came in haste for it.

Dromio of Ephesus: Money for me? Master, not a bit of money did I receive.

Antipholus of Ephesus: Did you not go to her for a bag of money?

Adriana: He came to me, and I delivered it to him.

Luciana: And I am witness with her that she did!

Dromio of Ephesus: God and the rope maker bear me witness that I was sent for nothing but a rope!

Pinch: Mistress, both man and master is mad! I know it by their pale and deadly looks. They must be bound and laid in some dark room.

Antipholus of Ephesus: Why did you lock me out, and why did you not send the money?

Adriana: I did not lock you out!

Dromio of Ephesus: And gentle master, I received no gold, but I confess, sir, that we were locked out.

Adriana: You villain, thou speakest false in both!

Antipholus of Ephesus: And you are false in every way.

(Tries to strike Adriana.)

Adriana: O bind him, bind him! Let him not come near me!

Pinch: Help! Help! The fiend is strong within him!

Luciana: Ay me, poor man. How pale and wan he looks!

(Enter three men to bind Antipholus of Ephesus.)

Antipholus of Ephesus: What, will you kill me? You, officer, I am thy prisoner.

Officer: Masters, let him go. He is my prisoner and you shall not have him.

Pinch: Go bind this man for he is frantic, too!

(The three men bind Dromio of Ephesus.)

Adriana: Good Master Doctor, see that he is safely brought home to my house. O most unhappy day! (Exit Doctor Pinch with the three men dragging out Antipholus of Ephesus and Dromio of Ephesus.) Say now, who ordered him to be arrested?

Officer: One Angelo, a goldsmith. Do you know him?

Adriana: I know the man. What is the sum my husband owes?

Officer: Two hundred ducats.

Adriana: For what?

Officer: For a chain your husband had him make for him.

Adriana: He did speak of giving me a chain, but I have it not.

Woman: Your husband, all in rage, today came to my house and took away my ring—the ring I saw upon his finger now. Straight after did I meet him with a chain.

Adriana: It may be so, but I never did see it. Come officer, bring me where the goldsmith is. I long to know the truth of all this.

(Enter Antipholus of Syracuse and Dromio of Syracuse with swords drawn.)

Luciana: God, for thy mercy! They are loose again!

Adriana: And come with naked swords! Let us call for more help to have them bound again.

Officer: Away! They will kill us!

(Exit Adriana, Luciana, and the Officer.)

Antipholus of Syracuse: I see they are afraid of swords.

Dromio of Syracuse: She that would be your wife, now ran from you.

Antipholus of Syracuse: I will not stay here tonight for all the town. Therefore away, to get our stuff aboard.

Scene 9: In Front of an Abbey About Five O'clock
(Angelo and the Merchant enter.)

Angelo: I am sorry, sir, that I have hindered you so, but I am positive I gave him the chain, though most dishonestly he doth deny it.

Merchant: What reputation does he have here in the city?

Angelo: A very good reputation, and very highly beloved. He is second to none that lives here in the city.

Merchant: Speak softly. Yonder, I think he walks.

(Enter Antipholus of Syracuse and Dromio of Syracuse.)

Angelo: It is he, and that golden chain about his neck which he denied having. Stay close by for I will speak to him. Signor Antipholus, I wonder much that you would put me to this shame and trouble. This chain which you now wear so openly, can you deny having it?

Antipholus of Syracuse: I never did deny having it.

Merchant: Yes you did, and wore to it too!

Antipholus of Syracuse: Who heard me deny it or swear to it?

Merchant: These ears of mine heard you. Fie on thee! 'Tis a pity thou livest to walk where honest men live.

Antipholus of Syracuse: Thou art a villain to speak thus. I'll prove my honesty against thee presently, if you dare stand up to me!

(They draw swords. Enter Adriana, Luciana, Woman, and citizens of the town of Ephesus.)

Adriana: Hold! Hurt him not, for God's sake! He is mad! Take his sword away and bind Dromio, too, and carry them to my house.

Dromio of Syracuse: Run, master, run! Find a place to hide. Here is a priory, a religious house . . . In, or we are lost!

(Antipholus of Syracuse and Dromio of Syracuse run into the abbey. Enter the Abbess.)

Abbess: Be quiet, people. Why do you gather here?

Adriana: To get my poor distracted husband. Let us come in, that we may find him fast and carry him home to recovery.

Angelo: I knew he was not in his perfect wits.

Merchant: I am sorry now that I did draw my sword.

Abbess: How long has he been in this condition?

Adriana: This week he hath been heavy, sour, sad, and much different from the man he was.

Abbess: Has he lost much wealth? Buried some dear friend?

Adriana: No, none of these. Good people, enter, and lay hold on him.

Abbess: No! Not a creature enters in my house!

Adriana: Then let your servants bring my husband out.

Abbess: Neither! He took this place for sanctuary, and he will not be touched till I have brought him to his wits again.

Adriana: I will not leave my husband here. It does not seem right to separate husband and wife!

Abbess: Be quiet and depart. Thou shalt not have him.

(Exits into the abbey.)

Luciana: Complain to the Duke about this.

Adriana: Come! I will throw myself at the Duke's feet and never rise till my tears and prayers have convinced him to get my husband away from the Abbess.

Merchant: I think the Duke comes in person himself for a death due to a sorry execution that will take place here.

Angelo: What is going to happen?

Merchant: To see a merchant from Syracuse beheaded publicly for daring to enter the city of Ephesus.

Angelo: See where they come. We will watch his death!

Luciana: Kneel to the Duke before he passes the abbey.

(Enter the Duke, old Aegeon, and officers.)

Duke: So, once again proclaim it publicly—if any friend will pay the sum for his ransom, he shall not die.

Adriana: Justice, most sacred Duke, against the Abbess!

Duke: The Abbess is a just and holy lady. It cannot be that she has done some wrong.

Adriana: May it please your Grace, Antipholus, my husband, had a most outrageous fit of madness. I had him bound, but he did escape. We come again to bind him, but he fled with his servant into the abbey, and here the Abbess shuts the gates in our faces and will not let us enter.

Duke: Go. Knock at the Abbey Gate! Bid the Lady Abbess come to me. I will settle this before I leave.

(Enter Adriana's servant.)

Luce: O mistress, mistress, run and save yourselves! My master and his servant have broken loose again. Unless you do something soon, they will kill somebody!

Adriana: Peace, fool . . . Thy master and his servant are in there!

(A loud cry is heard.)

Luce: Hark! I hear him Mistress. Fly, be gone!

Duke: Come, stand by me. Fear nothing. Men, be prepared to use your swords!

Adriana: Ay me! It is my husband!

(Enter Antipholus of Ephesus and Dromio of Ephesus.)

Antipholus of Ephesus: Justice, sweet Duke, against that woman! This day she shut the doors upon me!

Duke: A grievous fault! Say, woman, is this so?

Adriana: No, my good lord. Myself, he, and my sister today did dine together.

Luciana: She tells your highness the simple truth!

Angelo: These women lie! In this the man tells the truth! He dined not at home, but was locked out!

Duke: Did he have a golden chain of yours or not?

Angelo: He had, my lord. When he ran in here, these people saw the chain about his neck.

Merchant: Besides, I will swear that these ears of mine heard you confess you had the chain, and thereupon I drew my sword on you, and then you fled into this abbey here.

Antipholus of Ephesus: I never came within these abbey walls, nor ever did you draw your sword on me. I never saw the chain, so help me heaven!

Duke: You say he dined at home? The goldsmith here denies that saying. Sir, what say you?

Dromio of Ephesus: Sir, he dined with that woman.

Woman: He did, and from my finger snatched the ring.

Antipholus of Ephesus: 'Tis true my lord, this ring I had from her.

Duke: Did you see him enter the abbey here?

Woman: As sure as I see you standing there.

Duke: This is most strange. Go call the Abbess hither.
(Luce enters abbey to fetch Abbess.)
I think you are all stark mad!

Aegeon: Most mighty Duke, a word. Happily I see a friend that will save my life, and pay the sum that might set me free.

Duke: Speak freely, Syracusian.

Aegeon: Is not your name, sir, called Antipholus? And is not that your servant, Dromio? I am sure both of you remember me. Why look you so strange on me? You know me well!

Antipholus of Ephesus: I never saw you in my life till now.

Aegeon: O, grief hath changed me since you saw me last, but dost thou now know my voice?

Antipholus of Ephesus: Neither!

Aegeon: Dromio, nor thou?

Dromio of Ephesus: No sir.

Aegeon: I am sure you do!

Dromio: And I am sure I do not!

Aegeon: In seven short years my son has forgotten me. Tell me thou art my son, Antipholus!

Antipholus of Ephesus: I never saw my father in my life.

Aegeon: Seven years ago in Syracuse we were parted, but perhaps thou art ashamed to acknowledge me in such misery.

Antipholus of Ephesus: The Duke and all that know me in the city can witness with me that it is not so. I never saw Syracuse in my life.

Duke: I will verify that Antipholus of Ephesus has never been to Syracuse.

(Enter Abbess with Antipholus of Syracuse and Dromio of Syracuse.)

Abbess: Most mighty Duke, behold a man so wronged.

Adriana: I see two husbands, or mine eyes deceive me!

Duke: Which is the natural man, and which the spirit?

Dromio of Syracuse: I, sir, am Dromio. Command him away!

Dromio of Ephesus: I, sir, am Dromio. Pray, let me stay!

Antipholus of Syracuse: Aren't you Aegeon or else his ghost?

Dromio of Syracuse: O, my old master, who has bound you so?

Abbess: Whoever bound him, I will loose his bonds and gain a husband by his liberty. Speak, old Aegeon, if you are the man that once had a wife called Aemilia that gave birth to twin sons. If thou be'st the same Aegeon, speak then, and speak to your Aemilia.

Aegeon: Aemilia! (They embrace.) Tell me, where is that son that floated with thee on the fatal raft?

Abbess: What became of them I know not!

Duke: Why, here begins this morning story right. These two Antipholuses, these two so like, and these two Dromios. These are the parents to these children, which accidentally are met together!

Antipholus of Syracuse: No sir, not I. I came from Syracuse.

Duke: Stay, stand apart. I know not which is which!

Antipholus of Ephesus: I originally came from Corinth, my most gracious lord.

Dromio of Ephesus: And I with him!

Adriana: Which of you did dine with me today?

Antipholus of Syracuse: I, gentle mistress!

Adriana: And are you not my husband?

Antipholus of Syracuse: I am not!

(Adriana nearly faints.)

Angelo: That is the chain which you received from me, is it not?

Antipholus of Syracuse: I think it be, sir.

Antipholus of Ephesus: And you, sir, for this chain arrested me?

Angelo: I think I did, sir. I deny it not!

Adriana: I sent you money for your bail, sir, by Dromio, but I think he brought it not!

Dromio of Ephesus: No, none by me!

Antipholus of Syracuse: This purse of ducats I received from you, and Dromio my man did bring it to me.

Antipholus of Ephesus: This purse I use to ransom my father's life!

Duke: It is not needed. Thy father hath his life.

Abbess: O renowned Duke, enter the abbey. Come to the feast after so long a grief.

Duke: With all my heart!

(Exit Abbess, Adriana, Luciana, Angelo, Merchant, and Duke. The citizens of Ephesus also leave.)

Dromio of Syracuse: Master, shall I fetch your things from the ship?

Antipholus of Ephesus: Dromio, what things of mine?

Antipholus of Syracuse: He speaks to me. I am your master, Dromio. Embrace thy brother there. Rejoice with him!

(Exit Antipholus of Syracuse and Antipholus of Ephesus.)

Dromio of Ephesus and Dromio of Syracuse: We came into the world like brother and brother, and now let's go hand in hand, not one before the other.

The Taming of the Shrew

Introduction

Shakespeare's *The Taming of the Shrew* will generate many moments of laughter. Every boy will want to play Petruchio, and every girl will want to be Katharine, but there are also many other amusing roles in this swift moving story. For instance, actors will have a delightful time portraying the roles of the helter-skelter servants, the comical, pompous father, Baptista, and the silly suitors in love with Katharine's sweet sister, Bianca. All the roles are clearly defined, so it is important to keep the pace rapid.

Staging

Scene 1
This scene takes place in a square in Padua. Have Lucentio and his servant, Tranio, enter down the aisle and hide near the stage as they overhear the family argument that ensues. When the family exits, the farcical aspects of the play begin when Lucentio and Tranio change clothes while the audience roars with laughter.

Scene 2
Stage this scene, which takes place in front of Hortensio's house, in front of the curtain. Petruchio and his servant make a loud entrance through the audience.

Scene 3
The curtain opens to a room in Baptista's house with the grand spectacle of Petruchio and Katharine fighting with each other. Don't attempt to stage the altercation, but rather let it take its natural course within reasonable limits.

Scene 4
Stage this scene at Baptista's house in front of the curtain. Have Petruchio make another noisy entrance down the center or side aisle in a ridiculous outfit. The wedding ceremony itself is performed in pantomime.

Scene 5
The curtain opens to a scene inside Petruchio's house. A table and two chairs are all the props that are required.

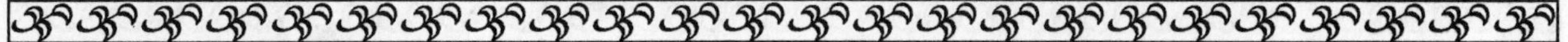

Allow plenty of room for flying vegetables and water spilling.

Scenes 6-7
Play these scenes in front of the curtain as the stage crew cleans up the mess on the stage.

Scenes 8-9
These roadside scenes can be staged in front of the curtain. It can be effective to have Katharine and Petruchio wander about the aisles of the auditorium as they have their comical argument.

Scene 10
The curtain opens to a full stage that is spotless with a table and chairs arranged for a banquet.

Costumes

The girls can wear long dresses. The boys can wear tights or tight trousers and fancy blouses with long sleeves. The rustic servants can prance about in tights and shirts or sweaters.

Vocabulary

Scene 1
achieve
beget
device
din
distinguished
dullard
endure
instruct
jesting
knowledge
lodging
longingly
pine
resolved
stark
stir
suitor
wits

Scene 2
access
artillery
assure
beauteous
beseech
boar
clang
curst
daunt
debt
dowries
effect
grateful
knavery
leisure
Methuselah
patron
profess
rage
renowned
scholar
shrew
sober

steeds
suffice
thither
tush
vile
woo

Scene 3

amazed
amiss
anxious
appearance
apt
array
assure
bestow
blunt
compliment
conclude
consented
contract
coy
cuff
envy
faith
flouts
grieved
hazel
heir
hue
incredible
kernels
lunatic
lute
meddle
modest
nightingale
orchard
ply
proceed
provide
rails
regard
ruffian
slanderous
sole
sullen
survive
swat
tactful
unbind
waspish
witty
woo

Scene 4

breeches
chamber
content
detained
entreat
festival
impatient
opinion
resist
solemn
whim

Scene 5

campaign
conclusion
coverlet
fie
knaves
mutton
peasant
rogue
sermon
stirrup

Scene 6

affection
chattering
disguise

Scene 7

arrogance
bauble
cuffs
farthingales
finely
garments
giddy
merits
monstrous
ornaments
paltry
purses
repaid
ruffs
spites
tormenting
tripe

Scene 8	tarry	vow
grandsire	temperamental	withered
henceforth		

Scene 9	midst	wrought
dower	offended	yonder
match	undone	

Scene 10	crowns	mistress
assurance	enslaved	personality
banquet	headstrong	sovereign
commits	intolerable	vile
craves	marks	wager

Characters

Baptista, rich gentleman of Padua
Katharine, his eldest daughter
Bianca, his youngest daughter
Lucentio, in love with Bianca
Petruchio, suitor to Katharine
Gremio, suitor to Bianca
Hortensio, suitor to Bianca
Tranio, servant to Lucentio
Grumio, servant to Petruchio
Curtis, servant to Petruchio
Nathaniel, servant to Petruchio
Philip, servant to Petruchio
Joseph, servant to Petruchio
Nicholas, servant to Petruchio
Widow
Tailor
Haberdasher
Servants
Very old man

The Taming of the Shrew

Scene 1: A Square in Padua
(Enter Lucentio and Tranio.)

Lucentio: Ah, good servant, here we are in Padua at last. I can hardly wait to begin my studies. O, how I thirst for knowledge.

Tranio: Gentle master, I am glad that you wish to improve your mind, and glad I am that your father is wealthy enough to afford to send you here to Padua for that very purpose. But, good master, let us not forget that all work and no play doth make Jack a dullard. In brief, sir, you owe it to yourself to take some amusement.

Lucentio: Tranio, thou dost advise me well. Let's go and take a lodging fit to entertain such friends as time in Padua shall beget. (Enter Baptista with Katharine, Bianca, Gremio, and Hortensio.) But stay while, what company is this?

Tranio: Master, some show to welcome us to town.

Baptista: (To Gremio and Hortensio.)
Gentlemen, beg me no further, for I am firmly resolved not to allow my youngest daughter to be married before I have a husband for her elder sister. If either of you love Katharine, you have my permission to court her at your pleasure.

Gremio: No thanks! She's too rough for me. Hortensio, will you marry her?

Katharine: (To Baptista.)
Father, is it your will to make a fool of me amongst these fools?

Hortensio: Fools, maid, how mean you this? Not fools enough to marry you, unless you were much gentler than you are.

Katharine: In faith, sir, never fear. I'll never marry such as you. But slap your face I will, if you should but ask!

Hortensio: From all such devils, good Lord, deliver us!

Gremio: And me too, good Lord!

Tranio: (Aside to Lucentio.)
Master, here's some good pastime. The girl is stark mad or just plain forward.

Lucentio: (Aside to Tranio.)
But her sister is very sweet tempered. Let's be quiet and listen.

Tranio: (Aside to Lucentio.)
Well said, master.

Baptista: Gentlemen, I mean what I have said. Bianca, go in the house, and let it not displease you, good Bianca, for I will love you none the less, my girl.

Katharine: A fine thing!

Bianca: It's all right, dear father. My books will keep me company.

Lucentio: (Aside to Tranio.)
Listen Tranio, doesn't she have a pretty voice?

Hortensio: Signor Baptista, surely you are jesting!

Gremio: Why will you sacrifice Bianca's happiness, Signor Baptista, for this fiend of hell? Why make Bianca wait to get married?

Baptista: I'm sorry gentlemen, my mind is made up. Go in, Bianca. (Exit Bianca.) I know she likes music and poetry, so I will get tutors to instruct her. If you, Hortensio, or Signor Gremio, know any such tutors, send them to me and I will pay them well to instruct mine own children in good bringing-up. And so farewell. Katharine, you may stay here, for I have more to say to Bianca.

(Baptista exits.)

Katharine: Why, I will go too!

(Katharine exits.)

Gremio: You are so bad tempered! No one will care! Well, Hortensio, I guess we'll just have to wait. Farewell, yet for the love I bear sweet Bianca, if I can find a man who will be her tutor, I will send him to her father.

Hortensio: So will I, Signor Gremio. But just a moment. Even though we are rivals for Bianca's love, there is one thing in which we should cooperate.

Gremio: What's that, I pray?

Hortensio: Why, sir, to get a husband for her sister Katharine, of course!

Gremio: A husband? A devil!

Hortensio: I say a husband.

Gremio: I say a devil. Hortensio, do you think, though her father is a very rich man, any man is so foolish as to be married to such a woman?

Hortensio: Tush, Gremio. Though it's beyond patience and mind to endure her screaming, there are good fellows in the world that would take her with all her faults because she is rich.

Gremio: I don't know. I had as soon be whipped every morning before breakfast.

Hortensio: As you say, there's small choice in rotten apples. But by helping Baptista's eldest daughter get a husband we set his youngest free for a husband. Sweet Bianca! Then we can be rivals! Till then, let's join hands. All right?

Gremio: Agreed! And I will give the best horse in Padua to the man who'll woo her and wed her and rid the house of her. Come on!

(Exit Gremio and Hortensio.)

Tranio: I pray, sir, tell me, is it possible that love should of a sudden take such hold?

Lucentio: O Tranio, till now I never thought it possible or likely. But see, while I stood looking on I do confess to thee I burn, I pine, I perish, Tranio, if I cannot win this young modest girl. Advise me, Tranio, for I know you can. Help me, Tranio, for I know you will.

Tranio: Master, it is not time to scold you now, but you looked so longingly on the maid, perhaps you didn't notice . . .

Lucentio: O yes, I saw sweet beauty in her face.

Tranio: Saw you no more? Marked you not how her sister began to scold and raise such a storm that mortal ears might hardly endure the din?

Lucentio: Tranio, I saw her coral lips move, and with her sweet breath she did perfume the air. Everything sweet was all I saw in her.

Tranio: Nay, then 'tis time to stir him from his trance. I pray awake, sir, if you love the maid, bend thoughts and wits to achieve her. Thus it stands. Her eldest sister is such a shrew, that till the father rid his hands of her, master, your love must wait. But the trouble is, she will not be annoyed with suitors.

Lucentio: Ah, Tranio, what a cruel father he is! But didn't you notice, he took some care to get her school masters to instruct her?

Tranio: Yes sir.

Lucentio: I have it, Tranio.

Tranio: Master, two minds with the same plot!

Lucentio: Tell me thine first.

Tranio: You will be the schoolmaster, and undertake the teaching of the maid. That's your device.

Lucentio: It is! Can I get away with it, do you think?

Tranio: Not possible. For who shall act your part and be in Padua here as Vincentio's son, keep house and ply his books, welcome his friends, visit his countrymen and banquet them?

Lucentio: Ah . . . ha! I'll tell you. We have not been seen anywhere, nor can we be distinguished by our faces for man or master. Then it follows thus. *You* shall be master in my place, keep house and servants, as I should. I will be some Florentine, some Neopolitan, or a man from Pisa.

'Tis hatched and shall be so. Tranio, undress. Take my colored hat and cloak.

(They change clothes.)

Tranio: Since it is your pleasure, sir, I must obey. I promised your father to be serviceable to his son, although I think it was in another sense. I am content to be Lucentio, because so well I love Lucentio.

Lucentio: Hurry! Let me pretend to be a teacher for that maid, Bianca, whose sudden sight hath thrilled my heart. Oh, one more thing . . . I want you to pretend to be another suitor for Bianca's hand. Don't ask me why, my reasons are both good and weighty.

Scene 2: In Front of Hortensio's House an Hour Later
(Enter Petruchio and Grumio.)

Petruchio: This is my good friend, Hortensio's house. Yes, I recognize it. Knock on the door.

Grumio: What, sir?

Petruchio: Pay attention! Knock on the door, I say!

Grumio: Which door, sir?

Petruchio: Why, Hortensio's door!

Grumio: Which door is that?

Petruchio: I'll show you, you fool!

(Wrings Grumio by the ear.)

Grumio: Help! Help! My master is mad!

Petruchio: Now knock when I bid, you villain.

(Enter Hortensio.)

Hortensio: How now, what's the matter? Why, it's my good friend, Petruchio.

Petruchio: Hortensio! How are you?

Hortensio: Petruchio! Tell me now, what happy wind blows you to Padua from old Verona?

Petruchio: Well, Hortensio, my father died recently and left me pretty well off, and so I decided that it was time I got married and settled down. But first, I have come abroad to see the world.

Hortensio: Well, I am glad to see you. You haven't changed a bit.

Grumio: No sir, he sure has not.

Petruchio: Be gone or else be quiet, I warn you! Hortensio, do you know of any marriageable women with large dowries? I've come to Padua to get a wealthy wife.

Hortensio: No, I don't . . . well . . . yes . . . I do know such a female, and I promise you she is rich, very rich. But you are too much my friend, and I'll not wish her on you.

Petruchio: Hortensio, between friends few words suffice, and therefore, if you know a woman rich enough to be Petruchio's wife, be she as ugly as sin, as old as Methuselah, I don't care. I'll marry her . . . *if* she's rich enough.

Grumio: 'Tis true, sir he tells you flatly what his mind is. Why, give him gold enough and marry him to a woman without a tooth in her head, it does not matter. Nothing matters to him but money!

Hortensio: Petruchio, I was only joking. I could help thee to a wife with wealth enough, and young and beauteous, brought up as best becomes a gentlewoman. Her only fault, and that is fault enough, is that she has a vile temper beyond all reason. Even if I were poor as a church mouse, I would not wed her for a mine of gold.

Petruchio: Quiet, Hortensio! Thou knowest not gold's effect. Tell me her father's name, and 'tis enough. For I will woo her though she howl as loud as thunder.

Hortensio: Her father is Baptista Minola, a pleasant and courteous gentleman. Her name is Katharine Minola, renowned in Padua for her scolding tongue.

Petruchio: I know her father! And he knew my father well! I will not sleep, Hortensio, until I have met her, and therefore excuse me if I leave you, unless you will accompany me hither.

Hortensio: Oh no, Petruchio . . . I can't let you.

Grumio: I pray you, sir, let him go while the humour lasts. On my word, if she knew him as well as I do, she would think scolding would do little good upon him. He's a match for any woman's temper! You know him not, sir.

Hortensio: But . . . O, all right. However, I must go with you, for I'm in love with Baptista's younger daughter Bianca, beautiful Bianca. And he withholds her from me and other suitors till Katharine the curst has got a husband.

Grumio: Katharine the curst! That's a title for a maid!

Hortensio: Now, my friend, will you do me a favor? I want you to introduce me disguised in sober robes to old Baptista as a music teacher. I'll instruct Bianca, that so I may by this device at least have leave and leisure to secretly court her.

Grumio: Here's knavery! See how the young folks put their head together to fool the old folks.

Petruchio: Very well! Make haste and disguise yourself!

(Enter Gremio and Lucentio disguised as Cambio, a schoolmaster.)

Grumio: Master, master, look about you. What goes here?

Hortensio: Quiet, Grumio, it is the rival of my love. Petruchio, let's stand by awhile and listen.

Gremio: O very well, I have read the note. But listen, sir, I'll have you read no other love letters to her, you understand me? (Smells the note.) Ah, very well perfumed, but Bianca is sweeter than perfume itself. What will you teach her?

Lucentio: I assure you, whatever I read to her, I'll plead for you as my patron as firmly as you would yourself, and perhaps with more successful words than you, unless you were a scholar, sir.

Gremio: O this learning . . . bah!

Grumio: (Aside.)
He's not very bright is he!

Petruchio: Quiet!

Hortensio: Ssshh. Quiet! (Comes forward.) God save you, Signor Gremio.

Gremio: And you are well met, Signor Hortensio. Do you know where I am going? To Baptista Minola. I promised to look for a tutor for the fair Bianca, and by good fortune I have found this young man. He is well read in poetry and other books, good ones I'm sure.

Hortensio: Good! And I have met a fine musician to instruct fair Bianca, who is so beloved of me.

Gremio: Beloved of *me,* and that my deed shall prove!

Hortensio: Gremio, 'tis now no time to argue. Listen to me. I'll tell you wonderful news. Here is a gentleman whom I met by chance. He will undertake to woo curst Katharine! Yea, and to marry her, if her dowry pleases him.

Gremio: That's wonderful, if he'll do it. Hortensio, have you told him all her faults?

Petruchio: I know she is a shrew. If that is all, masters, I fear no harm.

Gremio: No, friend? Where are you from?

Petruchio: Born in Verona, old Antonio's son. My father dead, my fortune lives for me, and I do hope good days and long to see.

Gremio: O sir, such a life, with such a wife, were strange. But if you have a stomach for it, you shall have my assistance. But will you woo this wild cat?

Petruchio: Certainly! That's why I came here. Do you think a little din can daunt mine ears? Have I not in my time heard lions roar? Have I not heard the sea rage like an angry boar? Have I not heard heaven's artillery thunder in the skies? Have I not in a pitched battle heard neighing steeds and trumpet's clang? Screaming from a woman will not stop me. Tush, tush, sir!

Grumio: He fears nobody!

Hortensio: I promised we could split the cost of his wooing, no matter how costly.

Gremio: And so we will, provided he wins her.

Grumio: I would I were as sure of a good dinner.

(Enter Tranio dressed as Lucentio.)

Tranio: Gentlemen, God save you. If I may be so bold tell me, I beseech you, what is the shortest way to the house of Signor Baptista Minola?

Gremio: He that has two fair daughters, is that who you mean?

Tranio: Even he.

Gremio: Hark you, sir, you don't mean to see her, do you?

Tranio: Perhaps him and her, sir. What have you to do with it?

Petruchio: Oh sir, he means no harm.

Tranio: Well, I don't like busy bodies.

Lucentio: (Aside.)
Well begun, Tranio.

Hortensio: Sir, a word ere you go. Are you a suitor to the maid you talk of, yea or no?

Tranio: And if I am, sir, what of it?

Gremio: Nothing! If without more words you will go.

Tranio: Why sir, I pray, are not the streets as free for me as for you?

Gremio: But *she* is not!

Tranio: For what reason, I beseech you.

Gremio: Because I'm going to marry her!

Hortensio: That's what he thinks! I'm the one she'll choose!

Tranio: Please, gentlemen! She may have a thousand suitors, then one more won't make any difference.

Hortensio: Sir, let me be so bold as to ask you, did you ever see Baptista's daughter?

Tranio: No, sir, but hear I do that he hath two . . . the one as famous for a scolding tongue as is the other for her beauty.

Petruchio: Sir, sir, the first one is for me. Let her go by.

Gremio: Yea, leave that labour to great Hercules!

Petruchio: Sir, the youngest daughter is kept from all access of suitors and her father will not allow her to be engaged until the older sister be wed, and not before.

Tranio: If it be so, sir, that you are the man that breaks the ice and marry the elder thus setting the younger free, we'll all be in your debt!

Hortensio: Sir, you say well, and since you do profess to be a suitor, you must as we do help us pay this gentleman's expenses.

Tranio: Agreed! Let us eat and drink as friends!

Grumio: An excellent idea! Fellows, let's be gone.

Hortensio: Petruchio, we shall be forever grateful!

Scene 3: A Room in Baptista's House That Afternoon

(Bianca's hands are tied together and she is pleading with Katharine.)

Bianca: Good sister, please unbind my hands!

Katharine: Tell me, of all thy suitors whom thou lovest best. Don't lie!

Bianca: Believe me, sister, I have not yet seen that special face which I could fancy more than any other.

Katharine: That's a lie! Is it not Hortensio you love best?

Bianca: If you're in love with him, sister, I swear I'll plead for you myself, and you shall have him.

Katharine: O then, perhaps you fancy riches more? You will choose Gremio to keep you fair.

Bianca: Is it for him you do envy me so? Nay, then you jest, and now I see you have but jested with me all this while. Please, sister, Kate, untie my hands.

Katharine: If that be jest, then all the rest was so.

(Katharine strikes Bianca. Enter Baptista.)

Baptista: Katharine! Stop! Bianca, stand aside. Poor girl she weeps. Go ply your needle, meddle not with her. For shame, you devilish spirit, why dost thou wrong her that never wronged thee? When did she ever cross thee with a bitter word?

Katharine: Her silence flouts me, and I'll be revenged!

(Attempts to strike Bianca.)

Baptista: (Holds Kate back.)
What, in my sight? Bianca, get thee in.

(Bianca exits.)

Katharine: So, you won't let me touch your precious Bianca? She is your favourite. The devil take Katharine the curst, but find a husband for sweet Bianca. I will go weep till I can find a chance for revenge.

(Katharine exits.)

Baptista: Was ever a gentleman thus grieved as I? But who comes here?

(Enter Gremio with Lucentio as a tutor, Petruchio with Hortensio as a tutor, and Tranio dressed as Lucentio.)

Gremio: Good morrow, neighbor Baptista.

Baptista: Good morrow, neighbor Gremio. God save you, gentlemen.

Petruchio: And you, sir, pray have you not a daughter called Katharine, fair and charming?

Baptista: I have a daughter, sir, called Katharine.

Gremio: You are too blunt. Be more tactful.

Petruchio: Sir, I have heard of her beauty, her friendliness, her bashfulness, and her mild behavior, and so I've been bold enough to come and see for myself, and for my welcome to your house, I present you with a teacher for your daughter. (Petruchio presents Hortensio.) He can teach her music and mathematics. Will you accept him, sir?

Baptista: You're welcome, sir, and he too is welcome. But for my daughter Katharine, this I know, she is not for you . . . more's the pity.

Petruchio: I see, you do not mean to part with her, or else you don't like my appearance.

Baptista: You mistake me, sir. What is your name?

Petruchio: Petruchio is my name, Antonio's son. A man well known throughout all of Italy.

Baptista: I knew him well. You are welcome for his sake.

Gremio: Please, Petruchio. I pray, let me get in a word. Goodness, you are forward.

Petruchio: Pardon me, Signor Gremio, but I want to get going.

Gremio: Neighbor, I also have a gift for you. I present unto you this young scholar. (Presents Lucentio.) He has been studying Greek, Latin, and other languages. His name is Cambio. Pray accept his service.

Baptista: A thousand thanks, Signor Gremio. Welcome, good Cambio. (To Tranio.) But gentle sir, you're a stranger. May I be so bold as to know the cause of your coming?

Tranio: Pardon me, sir, the boldness is mine own that, being a stranger in this city, do make myself a suitor to your daughter Bianca, even though you have resolved to marry your eldest daughter first. All that I request is that I may be welcomed among the rest that woo Bianca and, toward the education of your daughters, I here bestow this small packet of Greek and Latin books. Will you accept them?

Baptista: Lucentio is your name? From where I pray?

Tranio: From Pisa, sir, son to Vincentio.

Baptista: The richest man in Pisa by report. I know him well. You are very welcome, sir. (To Hortensio and Lucentio.) You take the lute, and you the set of books. You shall go see your pupils presently. Servant, lead these gentlemen to my two daughters, and tell them both these are their tutors. Bid them to use them well. (Exit servant with Hortensio and Lucentio.) We will walk a little in the orchard and then to dinner.

Petruchio: Signor Baptista, I am anxious to begin. It isn't every day I come to woo. You knew my father well, and he left me sole heir to all his lands and goods. Then tell me, if I get your daughter's love, what is her dowry?

Baptista: After my death, half of my lands and twenty thousand gold pieces.

Petruchio: And, for that dowry, I'll assure her, if she survive me, of all my lands and leases whatsoever. Let's draw up a contract between us.

Baptista: Ay, when you have won Katharine's love. For that comes first.

Petruchio: Why, that is nothing. For I tell you, father, I am rough and woo not like a babe.

Baptista: Well, my good wishes, but be prepared for some unhappy words.

Petruchio: Never fear.

(Enter Hortensio with a wounded head.)

Baptista: How now, my friend. Why do you look so pale?

Hortensio: If I look pale, it's because Katharine hit me!

Baptista: What, will my daughter prove a good musician?

Hortensio: I think she'll sooner prove a soldier. Iron may hold with her, but never lutes.

Baptista: Why, canst thou not break her to the lute?

Hortensio: No, for she has broke the lute to me. She struck me on the head with it, and there I stood amazed!

Petruchio: Now, by the world, there is a healthy wench. I love her ten times more than I did before. How I long to chat with her.

Baptista: Tutor, proceed in practice with my younger daughter. She's apt to learn and be thankful for good teaching. Signor Petruchio, will you come with me, or shall I send my daughter Kate to you?

Petruchio: Send her to me! (Exit all except Petruchio.) I'll woo her with some spirit when she comes. If she rails, why then I'll tell her she sings as sweetly as a nightingale. If she frowns, I'll say she smiles. If she do bid me go out, I'll give her thanks as though she bid me stay by her a week. If she deny to wed, I'll set the wedding date. (Enter Katharine.) But here she comes! And now, Petruchio, speak! Good morrow, Kate, for that's your name I hear.

Katharine: Well, you heard wrong or you're hard of hearing. They call me Katharine who do talk of me.

Petruchio: You lie, in faith, for you are called plain Kate, and therefore Kate, I am moved to woo you for my wife.

Katharine: Moved? In good time. Let him that moved you hither remove you hence! I knew you at the first to be a moveable idiot!

Petruchio: Thank you for the pretty compliment. Now, come sit on my lap.

Katharine: Who! Me?

Petruchio: It's all right, Kate. You are not too heavy. You are young and light.

Katharine: Too light for such as you to catch, and yet as heavy as my weight should be.

Petruchio: Come, come you wasp. In faith, you are too angry.

Katharine: If I be waspish, best beware my sting.

Petruchio: The way to handle a wasp is to give it a swat!

Katharine: You wouldn't dare! Get out!

Petruchio: What? So soon? Nay, come again. Good Kate, I am a gentleman.

Katharine: We'll see about that!

(She slaps Petruchio.)

Petruchio: I swear I'll cuff you, if you strike again.

Katharine: If you strike me, you are no gentleman.

Petruchio: Nay come, Kate, come, you must not look so sour.

Katharine: It is my fashion when I see a crab.

Petruchio: Why here's no crab, and therefore look not sour.

Katharine: There is, there is!

Petruchio: Then show it to me!

Katherine: If I had a mirror, I would.

Petruchio: What, you mean my face?

Katharine: Well aimed of such a young one.

Petruchio: Now, by Saint George, I am too young for you.

Katharine: Too young! Then why are you so wrinkled?

Petruchio: 'Tis with cares.

Katharine: I care not.

(Attempts to leave.)

Petruchio: O no, you don't.

(Petruchio grabs Katharine and they begin to wrestle.)

Katharine: Let me go!

Petruchio: Why? I find you very gentle. 'Twas told me you were rough and coy and sullen, and now I find that to be a lie. For you are pleasant, courteous, a bit slow in speech, but sweet as springtime flowers. You don't frown or bite the lip as angry girls do. You entertain me with gentle conduct. Why does the world report that Kate has a limp? O slanderous world, Kate like a hazel twig is straight and slender, and as brown in hue as hazel nuts, and sweeter than the kernels. O, let me see you walk. Why you don't limp!

Katharine: Go, fool!

Petruchio: Why you walk like a queen!

Katharine: Where did you study all this godly speech?

Petruchio: From my witty mother.

Katharine: A witty mother with a witless son.

Petruchio: Am I not wise?

Katharine: Too wise for your own good.

Petruchio: Katharine, let's get down to cases. In plain terms, your father has consented that you shall be my wife. Your dowry is agreed on and will you or not, I will marry you! Now, Kate, you have met your match for thy beauty makes me like you well. You must be married to no man but me, for I am he that's born to tame you, Kate, and bring you from a wild Kate to a gentle Kate. (Enter Baptista, Gremio, and Tranio.) Here comes your father. I must and will have Katharine for my wife.

Baptista: Now, Signor Petruchio, how goes it?

Petruchio: How but well, sir? How but well? It's impossible I should miss.

Baptista: My daughter, Katharine, why so sad?

Katharine: Don't call me daughter. Now, aren't you ashamed of yourself? You have showed a tender fatherly regard to wish me wed to a lunatic and a ruffian that thinks with curses to bluff his way in.

Petruchio: Father, 'tis thus, yourself and all the world that talked of her had talked amiss of her. If she be curst, it be play acting, for she's not forward, but modest as the dove. And to conclude, we have agreed so well together, that Sunday shall be the wedding day.

Katharine: I'll see thee hanged on Sunday first!

Gremio: Hark, Petruchio, she says she'll see thee hanged first.

Tranio: Well, there goes our good fortune.

Petruchio: Be patient, gentlemen. I choose her for myself. If she and I be pleased, what's that to you? The bargain between us two is that she shall still act angry in company. I tell you, it's incredible to believe how much she loves me. O the kindest Kate! She hung about my neck and kissed me so much that in a twink she won me for her love. You should see how tame she is when we are alone. Give me your hand, Kate. I will unto Venice go to buy my wedding clothes. Provide the feast, father, and invite the guests. I will be sure my Katharine shall be fine.

Baptista: I know not what to say, but give me your hands. God send you joy. Petruchio . . . 'tis a match!

Gremio and Tranio: Amen say we! We will be witnesses.

Petruchio: Father, and wife, and gentlemen, good-bye. I'm off to Venice. Sunday will come quickly. We will have rings and things and fine array, and kiss me Kate for we will be married on Sunday.

(Exits with Katharine.)

Gremio: Was ever a match made so quickly?

Baptista: I am dumbfounded!

Gremio: Now, Baptista, to your younger daughter. Now is the day we long have looked for. I am your friend and was suitor first.

Tranio: And I am the one that loves Bianca more than words can tell.

Gremio: You're too young for her!

Tranio: You're too old for her.

Baptista: Now I will decide this matter. He that can assure my daughter the greatest dower shall have my Bianca's love.

Tranio: He is old, I young.

Gremio: And may not young men die as well as old?

Baptista: Well, gentlemen, I am thus resolved. On Sunday, next you know my daughter Katharine is to be married. Now on Sunday following, Bianca shall be bride to one of you. And so I take my leave and thank you both.

Gremio: Good-bye.

Scene 4: Sunday at Baptista's House
(Enter all the wedding guests.)

Baptista: (To Tranio.)
This is the 'pointed day that Katharine and Petruchio should be married, and yet we hear not of our son-in-law. Where's the bridegroom? What say you to this shame of ours?

Katharine: No shame but mine! He wooed in haste and means to wed at leisure. I told you he was a fool. He'll woo as a husband, appoint the day of marriage, make feast, invite friends, and yet never means to get married at all. Now the world will point at me and say "Lo, there is mad Petruchio's wife . . . if it would please him come and marry her."

Tranio: Patience, good Katharine, and Baptista, too. Upon my life, Petruchio means well, Whatever holds him up, I know him to be honest.

Katharine: I wish I had never seen him!

(Exits weeping followed by Bianca.)

Baptista: Go, girl, I cannot blame thee for crying, for such an insult would vex a saint, much more a shrew of thy impatience.

(Enter servant, running.)

Servant: Master, master, old news! And such news as you never heard of?

Baptista: It is new and old, too! How may that be?

Servant: Why, is it not news to hear of Petruchio's coming?

Baptista: When he stands where I am, and sees you there.

Tranio: But say, what about the old news?

Servant: Why Petruchio is coming in a new hat, and an old jerkin, a pair of old breeches thrice turned, and riding an old broken down horse!

Tranio: O sir, be not angry. He often dresses in this fashion. It is a whim of his.

Baptista: I don't care how he's dressed, as long as he gets here.

Petruchio: (Offstage.)
Hey! Where is everybody? Isn't anybody at home?

(Enter Petruchio and Gremio.)

Baptista: You're welcome, sir.

Petruchio: And yet I come not well.

Tranio: Not as well dressed as I wish you were.

Petruchio: Were it not better I should rush in thus than come in no clothes? But where is Kate? Where is my lovely bride? How are you, father? (Slaps Baptista very hard on the back.) What's the matter? Why is everybody staring at me?

Baptista: Why, sir, you know this is your wedding day. First we were sad fearing you would not come, now sadder that you came dressed like this. Fie! Shame on you! An eyesore to our solemn festival.

Tranio: And tell us what has detained you so long?

Petruchio: O, it's a long story and a sad one, but the important thing is that I'm here. I'll tell you later why I was delayed, and you shall be satisfied. But where is Kate? I stay too long from her. The morning wears, 'tis time we were at church.

Tranio: See not your bride in clothes such as these. Go to my chamber for new robes.

Petruchio: Not I! I'll see her like this.

Baptista: But I trust you will not marry her like that!

Petruchio: Why, sir, is she marrying me or my clothes? If I could change myself as easily as I can change these clothes, that would be worth talking about. But what a fool am I to chat with you when I should bid good morrow to my bride, and seal the title with a lovely kiss.

(Exit Petruchio and Grumio.)

Tranio: He's up to something. If possible, we will persuade him to put on better clothes before he goes to the church.

Baptista: Too late. He comes with Katharine!

(The wedding ceremony takes place making Petruchio and Katharine man and wife. The local friar performs the simple ceremony of blessing the couple.)

Petruchio: Gentlemen and friends, I thank you for your pains. I know you expect to dine with me today and have prepared a great wedding feast, but my haste calls me home, and therefore here I mean to take my leave.

Baptista: Is it possible that you mean to leave now?

Petruchio: O, I must go before nightfall. I thank you all and so does my most patient, sweet, and gentle wife. Dine with my father-in-law, drink a health to me for I must go. Farewell to you all.

Tranio: Let me entreat you to stay till after dinner.

Petruchio: It may not be.

Gremio: Let me entreat you!

Petruchio: It cannot be.

Katharine: Let me entreat you.

Petruchio: I am content.

Katharine: Content to stay?

Petruchio: I am content that you should ask me to stay, but yet we will not stay.

Katharine: If you love me, stay!

Petruchio: Grumio, my horse.

Grumio: Ay, sir, they be ready, the oats have eaten the horses.

Katharine: Nay then, do as you wish. I will not go today, no, nor tomorrow . . . not till I please! The door is open, sir, there lies your way. You may go! For me, I'll not be gone till I please.

Baptista: Now, don't be angry, Kate!

Katharine: I will be angry! Father, be quiet! He shall stay till I'm ready.

Gremio: Ah-ha! Now it begins to work!

Katharine: Gentlemen, forward to the bridal dinner. I see a woman may be made a fool, if she had not the spirit to resist.

Petruchio: They shall go forward, Kate. Obey the bride, go to the feast, eat and drink full measure . . . be merry! But for my bonny Kate, she must go with me. Nay, look not big, nor stamp, nor stare, nor fret. I will be master of what is mine own. She is my wife. And here she stands, touch her whoever dare. I'll fight whoever tries to stop me. Grumio, draw forth thy weapon, we are beset by thieves. Rescue your mistress if thou be a man! Fear not, sweet wife, they shall not touch you, Kate. I'll protect you, Kate . . . I'll protect you against a million!

(Exit Petruchio dragging Katharine, followed by Grumio.)

Gremio: If they had not gone quickly, I would have died laughing.

Tranio: Of all mad matches never was the like.

Lucentio: Bianca, what's your opinion of your sister?

Bianca: I think she's well matched.

Baptista: Friends, though we lack bride and bridegroom, let us celebrate with a feast. Lucentio, you shall take the bridegroom's place, and let Bianca take her sister's place.

Lucentio: Shall sweet Bianca practice how to be a bride?

Baptista: She shall, Lucentio. Come, gentlemen!

Scene 5: Petruchio's House Late That Night

(Grumio enters.)

Grumio: Fie! Fie on all tired women, on all masters, and all foul way. Was ever man so beaten? Was ever man so weary? I am sent before to make a fire, and they are coming after to warm themselves. Hoooo! Curtis!

(Curtis enters.)

Curtis: Who is it that calls so coldly?

Grumio: A piece of ice. A fire, good Curtis.

Curtis: Is my master and his wife coming, Grumio?

Curtis: Is she such a shrew as reported?

Grumio: She was, good Curtis, before this frost. But thou knowest winter tames man, woman, and beast. But wilt thou make a fire, or shall I tell on you to our new mistress whose hand you'll soon feel for being slow!

Curtis: Please, Grumio, tell me how goes the world?

Grumio: A cold world, Curtis, and therefore fire. Do your duty, for my master and mistress are almost frozen to death.

Curtis: There's fire ready, and therefore, good Grumio, the news!

Grumio: I have caught a cold. Where's the cook? Is supper ready, the house clean, cobwebs swept, the carpets laid, and everything in order?

Curtis: All ready, and therefore I pray thee, news!

Grumio: First, know my horse is tired, my master and mistress fallen out.

Curtis: How?

Grumio: Out of their saddles into the dirt, and thereby hangs a tale. Lend thine ear. Now I begin. We came down a steep hill, my master riding behind my mistress . . . .

Curtis: Both on one horse?

Grumio: What's that to you? You tell the tale, and had you not interrupted me, you would have heard how her horse fell, and she under her horse. You would have heard in how muddy a place she fell, how he left her with the horse upon her, how he beat me because her horse stumbled, how she waded through the dirt to pull him off me, how he yelled at me, how I cried, how the horses ran away, how her bridle was burst, and many things which now you'll never know.

Curtis: By all this, he is more of a shrew than she!

Grumio: Ay, and that you'll find out when he comes home. But what talk I of this? Call forth Nathaniel, Joseph, Nicholas, Philip, Walter, Sugarsop, and the rest. Let their heads be slickly combed. Are they all ready?

Curtis: They are.

Grumio: Call them forth.

Curtis: Do you hear? Ho!

(Enter all the servants.)

Nathaniel: Welcome home, Grumio.

Philip: How are you, Grumio?

Joseph: Grumio.

Nicholas: Fellow Grumio.

Grumio: Now, my lads, is all ready, and all things neat?

Nathaniel: All is ready. How near is our master?

Grumio: He's just outside by now. Silence, I hear him!

(Enter Petruchio and Katharine.)

Petruchio: Where be these knaves? What, no man at the door to hold my stirrup? Nor to take my horse? Where is Nathaniel? Where is Gregory, Philip?

All Servants: Here, sir! Here, sir! Here, sir! Here, sir!

Petruchio: Here, sir! Here, sir! Here, sir! Here, sir! You logger-headed knaves. What, no attendance, no regard, no duty? Where is the fool I sent before?

Grumio: Here sir, as foolish as I was before.

Petruchio: You peasant! Did I not tell you to meet me in the park and to bring along these rascal knaves with you? Go rascals, go! Fetch me my supper! (Exit servants.) Sit down, Kate! And welcome! Food! Food! Food! (Enter servants with food.) Hurry I say! Nay, good sweet Kate, be merry. (To servants.) Off with my boots, you rogues. You villains, hurry! You twisted my ankle . . . out you rogue. Take that! (Strikes Nathaniel.) Be merry, Kate! Some water here. What ho! Where's my spaniel? Find him! (Exit Philip. Enter Nicholas with water.) Shall I have some water? Where are my slippers? Water! (Knocks over water.) You spilled it! You villains! (Strikes Nicholas.)

Katharine: Patience I pray you, 'twas an accident.

Petruchio: You are a beetle-headed, flap-eared knave! Come, Kate, sit down. I know you must be hungry. Will you give thanks, sweet Kate, or else shall I? What is this, mutton?

Joseph: Yes sir.

Petruchio: Who brought it?

Joseph: I

Petruchio: It's burnt! Where is the rascal cook? How dare you villains bring it and serve it to me? You know I hate it. Take it back, cups, plates, and all! (Throws food at servants.) You fools! Why do you grumble? I'll tend to you later!

(Exit servants on the run.)

Katharine: I pray you, husband, be not so angry. The meat was good enough I think.

Petruchio: I tell you it was burnt and dried up. It makes me sick, and it's not good for you. It's better that both of us go hungry than feed with such over-roasted flesh. Be patient, tomorrow we'll eat and for tonight we'll fast. Come, I will show you your bedroom.

(Exit Katharine and Petruchio. Re-enter servants.)

Nathaniel: Did you ever see the like!

Nicholas: He's killing her with kindness.

(Enter Curtis.)

Grumio: Where is he?

Curtis: In her room making a sermon to her. He claims that she, poor soul, doesn't know how to stand, to look, to speak, and says she sits with a slump. Shh—ahh—away, away, for he is coming.

(Exit all servants. Enter Petruchio.)

Petruchio: Thus have I begun my campaign, and it is my hope to have it end successfully. She ate no meat today, nor shall she eat none. Last night she slept not, nor tonight she shall not. As with meat, some fault I'll find about the making of the bed, and here I'll fling the pillow, this way the coverlet, another way the sheets, and all the time I'll pretend that all is done for her sake. And in conclusion she shall stay awake all night. And if she chance to doze, I'll keep her awake with complaints about the work of the servants. This is a way to kill a wife with kindness.

I'll curb her bad temper, if it's the last thing I'll do. He that knows better how to tame a shrew, now let him speak. I'll gladly listen.

Scene 6: In Front of Baptista's House Two Days Later
(Enter Tranio as Lucentio and Hortensio as Licio.)

Tranio: Is it possible, friend Licio, that Mistress Bianca doth fancy any other but Lucentio? I tell you sir, she loves me!

Hortensio: Sir, satisfy yourself in what I have said . . . stand by and listen. (Enter Bianca, and Lucentio as Cambio. They talk tenderly as they cross the stage and exit.) Now tell me, wasn't I right? Bianca loves none in the world so well as Cambio.

Tranio: O unconstant womankind! I tell thee, Licio, this is wonderful.

Hortensio: Let me tell you the truth. I am not Licio, nor a musician as I seem to be. This is a disguise. I am called Hortensio.

Tranio: Signor Hortensio, I have often heard of you and of your affection for Bianca, and since I see she loves another, I will with you forget Bianca and her love forever.

Hortensio: See how they kiss! Signor Lucentio, here is my hand, and here I firmly vow never to woo her more, but to forget her.

Tranio: I take the same oath! I wouldn't marry her even if she would beg me to! Fie on her . . . see how she caresses him!

Hortensio: For me, I will be married to a wealthy widow who has long loved me. And so farewell, Signor Lucentio. Kindness in woman, not their beautiful looks, shall win my love, and so I take my leave.

(Exit Hortensio. Re-enter Lucentio and Bianca.)

Tranio: Mistress Bianca, Master Lucentio . . . good news! Hortensio has decided that he no longer wishes to marry you.

Bianca: Ha-ha! And what of you, Tranio?

Tranio: O mistress, you jest! But yes, I too have given up the chase.

Lucentio: Well done, good Tranio. Then we are rid of him.

Tranio: In faith, he is going to marry a rich widow now that shall be wooed and wedded in a day.

Bianca: God give him joy.

Tranio: Ay, and he'll tame her.

Bianca: So *he* says, Tranio.

Tranio: Why not? He has gone to the taming school.

Bianca: The taming school? What, is there such a place?

Tranio: Yes mistress, and Petruchio is the teacher that teaches how to tame a shrew and quiet her chattering tongue.

Bianca: This is unbelievable.

(All exit.)

Scene 7: Petruchio's House That Afternoon
(Katharine and Grumio enter.)

Katharine: Did he marry me to starve me? Beggars that come to my father's door get more to eat! But I, who never knew how to beg, nor never needed it, am starved for meat, giddy for lack of sleep. And that which spites me more than all these wants, he does it under the name of perfect love. Please go get me something to eat. I care not what it is, as long as it's food.

Grumio: What say you to a pig's feet?

Katharine: 'Tis passing good, please let me have it.

Grumio: I fear it will not agree with you. How say you to a fat tripe finely broiled?

Katharine: I like it well, good Grumio. Fetch me some.

Grumio: I cannot tell. I fear it's not fresh. What say you to a piece of beef and mustard?

Katharine: A dish that I do love to feed upon.

Grumio: Ay, but the mustard is a little too hot!

Katharine: Why then the beef, and forget the mustard.

Grumio: Nay then I will not. You shall have the mustard or else you get no beef of Grumio.

Katharine: Then both, or one, or anything.

Grumio: Why then, the mustard without the beef?

Katharine: Out of here, you villain! (Strikes him.) You're only tormenting me. The whole pack of you! You feed my appetite, but you won't feed me! Get out of here!

(Enter Petruchio and Hortensio with meat.)

Petruchio: How fares my Kate? Aren't you feeling well?

Hortensio: Mistress, no cheer?

Katharine: I feel terrible!

Petruchio: Pluck up thy spirits. Look carefully upon me. Here, love, look what I've brought you. I prepared this meat myself. I am sure, sweet Kate, this kindness merits thanks. What, not a word? Nay then, you don't like it? Here take away this dish.

Katharine: No, please leave it.

Petruchio: The poorest service is repaid with thanks, and so shall mine before you touch the meat.

Katharine: I thank you, sir.

Petruchio: (Aside to Hortensio.)
Eat it up all, Hortensio, if you are a true friend. (To Katharine.) I hope it makes you feel better . . . Kate, eat! And now, my honey love, we will return to your father's house. We'll dress up and have a good time. We'll dress up with silken coats and caps and golden rings, with ruffs and cuffs, and farthingales and things. What, have you dined all ready? Good! The tailor is waiting to come in to show you a new dress I ordered. (Enter tailor.) Come tailor, let us see your ornaments. Lay forth the gown. (Enter haberdasher.) What's news with you, sir?

Haberdasher: Here is the cap your worship ordered.

Petruchio: Why, this was moulded on a midget's head. Fie! It is awful. Why 'tis a walnut shell, a toy, a trick, a baby's cap! Take it away. Let me have a bigger one.

Katharine: I'll have no bigger. This is in fashion and gentlewomen wear such caps as these.

Petruchio: When you are gentle, you shall have one, too, and not till then.

Hortensio: (Aside.)
That will not be soon.

Katharine: Why, sir, I trust I may have permission to speak, and speak I will. I am no child, no babe. I'll speak my mind! And if you cannot stand it, best you stop your ears.

Petruchio: What thou sayest is true. It is a paltry cap, a bauble, a silken pie. I love thee well, but . . .

Katharine: Love me or love me not, I like the cap, and it I will have, or I will have none.

Petruchio: Thy gown? Why, yes, come tailor, let us see it. O mercy, what stuff is here? What's this? A sleeve? 'Tis like a cannon! What in the devil do you call this?

Hortensio: (Aside.)
I see she's likely to have neither cap nor gown.

Tailor: You bid me make it according to the fashion and the time.

Petruchio: So I did. But if you remember, I did not bid you mar it to the time. I'll not have it!

Katharine: I never saw a better fashioned gown. Why, it is beautiful. You mean to make a fool of me!

Petruchio: Why true, he means to make a fool of thee!

Tailor: She says your worship means to make a fool of her, not I.

Petruchio: O monstrous arrogance! You lie! Away with this rag! I tell you that you've ruined her gown.

Tailor: Your worship is deceived. The gown is made just as Grumio gave order how it should be done.

Grumio: I gave him no order. I gave him the stuff.

Tailor: But how did you desire it should be made?

Grumio: With a needle and thread!

Tailor: But did you not request to have it cut?

Petruchio: Well, sir, in brief, the gown is not for me!

Grumio: You are in the right, sir, 'tis for my mistress.

Petruchio: Go take it away. (Aside to Hortensio.) Hortensio, see that the tailor is paid. (To the tailor.) Go! Take it away! Be gone and say no more!

Hortensio: (Aside to tailor.)
Tailor, I'll pay you for the gown tomorrow. Take no unkindness of his hasty words. Don't worry. (Loudly.) Away, I say!

(Exit tailor and haberdasher.)

Petruchio: Well, come, my Kate, we will go to your father's even in these honest plain clothes. Our purses shall be proud, our garments poor, for 'tis the mind that makes the body rich! If you're ashamed, you can say it's my fault, and therefore frolic. We will go at once to feast and sport us at your father's house. Go call my men and let us be off. Let's see, I think 'tis now about seven o'clock and we'll be there by dinner time.

Katharine: I assure you sir 'tis almost two and 'twill be supper time before we get there.

Petruchio: It will be seven, or I won't go! I will not go today, and before I do, it shall be what o'clock I say it is.

(Petruchio exits.)

Hortensio: So this is how one tames a shrew!

Scene 8: A Road Outside Padua Two Days Later
(Enter Tranio and Lucentio.)

Tranio: The old priest of St. Luke's Church is at your command at all hours.

Lucentio: And what of all this?

Tranio: Take Bianca to the church. I cannot tarry. I go to Saint Luke's to bid the priest be ready to marry you.

Lucentio: I will if she be so contented. And she will be pleased!

(Exit Tranio and Lucentio. Enter Petruchio, Katharine, Hortensio, and servants.)

Petruchio: Come, once more toward our father's. Good heavens, how bright and goodly shines the moon!

Katharine: The moon? The sun! It is broad daylight.

Petruchio: I say it is the moon that shines so bright.

Katharine: I know it is the sun that shines so bright.

Petruchio: Now, by my mother's son, and that's myself, it shall be moon, or star or whatever I say before I journey to your father's house.

Hortensio: (Aside to Katharine.)
Say as he says, or we shall never go on!

Katharine: Forward, I pray, since we have come so far and I'll say it is moon or sun, or whatever you please. And if you please to call it candle, henceforth I vow it shall be so for me.

Petruchio: I say it is the moon.

Katharine: I know it is the moon.

Petruchio: Then you lie. It is the blessed sun.

Katharine: Then it is the blessed sun, but sun it is not when you say it is not. And the moon changes even as your mind. And so it shall be for Katharine.

Petruchio: Well, well! Forward, forward. Let us go! (Enter an old man.) But soft, company is coming here. (To old man.) Good morrow, my good woman. Where are you going? Tell me, sweet Kate, and tell me truly too, hast thou seen a fresher gentlewoman? Such pink cheeks! Such beauty! And those two eyes become that heavenly face. Fair lovely maid, once more good day to you. Sweet Kate, embrace her for her beauty's sake.

Hortensio: (Aside.) It will make the man angry to make a woman of him.

Katharine: Young, fresh, fair, and sweet girl. Happy the parents of so fair a child.

Petruchio: Why, how now Kate. I hope thou art not mad! This is a man, old, faded, wrinkled, withered, and not a girl as you say he is.

Katharine: Pardon, old man, my mistaking eyes that have been so bedazzled by the sun that everything I look on seemeth green. Pardon, I pray for my mistake.

Petruchio: Do, good old grandsire, and bid us good-bye.

(Exit Petruchio and Katharine. Old man scratches his head and exits.)

Hortensio: Well Petruchio, this has given me new courage. Marry that widow, and if she be temperamental, then you have taught Hortensio how to handler her.

(Hortensio exits.)

Scene 9: A Street in Padua Half an Hour Later

(Enter Lucentio, Tranio, and Bianca.)

Tranio: Yonder he is, and we are all undone.

(Enter Baptista.)

Lucentio: Pardon, sweet father.

(Lucentio kneels.)

Hortensio: "Father!" What do you mean, sir?

Bianca: Pardon, dear father.

(Bianca kneels.)

Baptista: What do you mean? How hast thou offended Lucentio?

Lucentio: He's not Lucentio. I am he, that have by marriage made thy daughter mine. This is my servant, Tranio.

Baptista: Tranio? Thy servant? You are not Cambio?

Bianca: Cambio is changed into Lucentio.

Lucentio: Love wrought these miracles. Bianca's love made me exchange places with Tranio. What Tranio did I forced him to, then pardon him, sweet father, for my sake.

Baptista: Sir, your plainness and your honesty please me well, but what of her dower?

Lucentio: Dear sir, you know my father to be the wealthiest man in Pisa. I am his heir and only son. My wife and your daughter shall be the richest woman in all the land.

Baptista: How say you, Bianca, are you happy?

Bianca: O father, more than I can say.

Baptista: Then I am satisfied. The match is made and all is done.

(All exit. Enter Petruchio, Katharine, Grumio, and servants.)

Katharine: Wasn't that my father? Husband, let's follow.

Petruchio: First kiss me, Kate, and we will.

Katharine: What! In the midst of the street?

Petruchio: What! Art thou ashamed of me?

Katharine: No sir, but ashamed to kiss in public.

Petruchio: Why then, let's go back home. Come, away.

Katharine: Nay, I will give thee a kiss. (Kisses him.) Now pray thee, love, stay.

Petruchio: Is not this well? Come, my sweet Kate. Better once than never, for never too late.

(All exit.)

Scene 10: Lucentio's House That Evening

(Enter Baptista, Gremio, Lucentio, Bianca, Petruchio, Katharine, Hortensio, the widow, Grumio, Tranio, and servants.)

Lucentio: My fair Bianca, bid our father welcome. Brother Petruchio, sister Katharine, and thou Hortensio with thy loving widow, feast with us, and welcome to my house. My banquet is to close our stomachs up after our great good cheer. Pray you sit down, for now we sit to chat as well as eat.

(They all sit for the banquet.)

Petruchio: Nothing but sit and sit, and eat and eat!

Baptista: Padua affords this kindness, son Petruchio.

Petruchio: Padua affords nothing but what is kind.

Hortensio: For both our sakes, I would that were true.

Petruchio: Well, well, now on my life, Hortensio fears his widow.

Widow: Then never trust me, if I be afraid.

Petruchio: You misunderstand me. I mean Hortensio is afraid of you.

Widow: He that is giddy thinks the world turns round.

Katharine: Mistress, how mean you that? "He that is giddy thinks the world turns round." I pray you tell me what you meant by that.

Widow: Your husband being troubled by a shrew, measures my husband's wife by his own. And now you know my meaning.

Katharine: A very mean meaning.

Widow: Right. I mean you!

Katharine: And I am mean, indeed, respecting you!

(Katharine and the widow begin to fight.)

Petruchio: After her, Kate!

Hortensio: Get her, Widow!

Petruchio: A hundred marks, my Kate does put her down.

Hortensio: No, this is a time for merriment.

Petruchio: Spoken like a gentleman. Here's to thee, lad.

(Petruchio drinks to Hortensio. Katharine and the widow are still fighting.)

Baptista: Gremio, how do you like these witty folk?

Gremio: Believe me, sir, they are amusing.

Lucentio: A toast to my bride, Bianca.

(They all drink. Bianca separates the fighting pair.)

Bianca: Will you ladies accompany me?

(Exit Bianca, Katharine, and the widow.)

Baptista: Now, in good sadness, son Petruchio, I think thou hast the veriest shrew of all.

Petruchio: Well, I say no. And therefore, for assurance, let's each one send for his wife, and he whose wife is most obedient, to come at first when he sends for her, shall win the wager which we will propose.

Hortensio: An excellent idea. What shall we bet?

Lucentio: Twenty crowns.

Petruchio: Twenty crowns? Why I'd bet that money on my dog, but twenty times as much upon my wife.

Lucentio: A hundred then.

Hortensio: Agreed.

Petruchio: A match, 'tis done.

Hortensio: Who shall begin?

Lucentio: I will. Go, Tranio, bid your mistress come to me.

Tranio: Yes sir.

(Tranio exits.)

Baptista: Son, I'll bet your half that Bianca comes.

Lucentio: I'll have no halves. I'll pay it all myself. (Enter Tranio.) How now, what news?

Tranio: Sir, my mistress sends you word that she is busy, and cannot come.

Petruchio: How? She's busy and she cannot come? Is that an answer?

Hortensio: Sir, go and entreat my wife to come to me.

(Exit Tranio.)

Petruchio: Oh no! Entreat her! She then certainly will come.

Hortensio: I'm afraid, sir, do what you can, for *yours* will not be entreated. (Enter Tranio.) Now, where's my wife?

Tranio: She says you have some goodly jest in hand, she will not come. She bids you come to her.

Petruchio: Worse and worse, she will not come. O vile, intolerable, not to be endured. Grumio, go to your mistress and say I command her to come to me!

(Exit Grumio.)

Hortensio: I know her answer.

Petruchio: What?

Hortensio: She will not.

Petruchio: If so, then I lose the bet and that's the end of it.

(Enter Katharine.)

Baptista: Heavens above, here comes Katharine!

Katharine: What is it you will that you send for me?

Petruchio: Where is your sister, Bianca, and Hortensio's wife?

Katharine: They sit talking by the fire.

Petruchio: Go fetch them hither. If they refuse to come, force them to come. Away I say, and bring them here at once.

(Exit Katharine.)

Lucentio: Well, here is a wonder, if you talk of a wonder!

Hortensio: And so it is. I wonder what it means.

Petruchio: It means peace and love and a quiet life, and to the point, a very happy marriage.

Baptista: The wager thou hast won Petruchio, and I will add twenty thousand crowns to thy winnings, for she is changed as she had never been!

Petruchio: Nay, I will win my wager better yet, and show more sign of her obedience . . . her new personality and obedience. (Enter Katharine with Bianca and the widow.) See here she comes and brings your less thoughtful wives. Katharine, that hat of yours becomes you not. Off with the bauble and throw it under foot.
(Katharine obeys.)

Widow: Goodness, let me never have a husband that silly!

Bianca: What a foolish duty this is!

Lucentio: I wish your duty were as foolish too. The wisdom of your duty, fair Bianca, has cost me a hundred crowns since suppertime!

Bianca: The more fool you are for betting on my duty.

Petruchio: Katharine, tell these headstrong women what duty they owe their husbands.

Widow: Come, come now, you're joking! We will have no more telling.

Petruchio: Come, I say, and first begin with her.

Widow: She shall not!

Petruchio: I say she shall, and first begin with her!

Katharine: There, there, don't frown, it blots thy beauty. Thy husband is thy lord, thy life, thy keeper, thy head, thy sovereign, one that cares for thee and for thy maintenance, commits his body to painful work both by sea and land while thou liest warm at home, secure and safe. He craves no other reward but love, fair looks, and true obedience. Such duty a woman oweth to her husband. I am ashamed that women are so simple to offer war when they should kneel for peace. Ladies, place your hands in your husband's hand. My hand is ready to help him.

Petruchio: Now, that's a good wife! Come and kiss me, Kate!

Lucentio:	I can hardly believe my eyes!
Petruchio:	Come, Kate, say good night. We two are married, but you are enslaved. (To Lucentio.) 'Twas I who won the wager and you who lost the fight. And, being a winner, God give you a good night.
	(Exit Petruchio and Katharine.)
Hortensio:	Sleep well, Petruchio, for thou hast tamed a shrew.
Lucentio:	And with your help, Petruchio, we'll tame our women too!

The Tempest

Introduction

The Tempest is a challenging play to produce, but once involved, children will never forget Shakespeare's last complete play. *The Tempest* captures the simple beauty of living—its freedom, its forgiveness, and its laughter. It is a play full of magic that tells us that we are "such stuff as dreams are made on," from the lowly Caliban to the mighty Prospero. Good and evil are clearly defined.

Staging

Scene 1
This scene can be staged in front of the curtain. The curtain itself can billow in and blow out to represent the storm. Place a simple framework of a boat in front. Use very dim lighting and occasional flashes of lightning, which can be simulated by rapidly switching the lights on and off. Another way to depict the lashing storm is to use live students as waves. Bathing caps, bodies covered with pieces of blue and green cloth, and a host of arms attempting to engulf the ship will create an interesting effect. The storm can also be handled by presenting a series of large murals portraying various sequences of the poor little vessel's struggle to stay afloat.

Scene 2
The curtain opens on a magical island. Allow plenty of room for Ariel to "fly" about and Caliban to pounce and bounce in his frustrations. Caliban's hole can be offstage, and when he appears, there should be a long rope attached to his waist that is anchored off stage.

Scene 3
This scene can be staged in front of the curtain.

Scene 4
This is one of the funniest scenes from Shakespeare. The stage crew can produce thunder by rattling a sheet of metal or beating on a big drum. The scene can be also be staged in front of the curtain.

Scene 5
The curtain again opens to the magical island.

Scene 6
Stage this scene in front of the curtain.

Scene 7
Use the full stage for this scene. Ariel can cover the table with a piece of cloth to make the food disappear. Or, attach strong threads to the various items on the table and they will fly into the air when the strings are pulled by your stage manager and crew.

Scene 8
Make good use of the entire stage for this scene with characters going in and out. Prospero's tent can be an ordinary camping tent or two long pieces of cloth hung from the ceiling with an opening near the bottom. The spirits here, as in scene 7, are dancing figures with brown or black cloth draped around their faces. For the final speech, have Prospero step to the footlights as the curtain closes behind him and all the lights come on in the auditorium to take away the magic of the theater world.

Costumes

Prospero's cape should be something special—shiny, fluorescent, extremely delicate, or farfetched. Tunics and tights for the other characters will work fine. Invite children to suggest ideas for making Caliban look monster-like. Ariel's costume should be light and fragile. When he moves, he should seem to flutter.

Encourage actors to create their own music for the songs. Whenever Ariel is about, have a humming noise floating around the stage.

When Ariel is invisible he simply performs his actions behind the characters who are on the stage. Make sure that the other characters never look at Ariel. If you want to try a more complicated approach to Ariel's invisibility, use a roaming spotlight on stage and have Ariel speak his lines through a microphone off stage.

Vocabulary

Scene 1

acre
assist
authority
barren
bawling
boatswain
comfort
councillor
exile
fate
incharitable
merely
pox
rascal
topmast
topsail

Scene 2

abducted
abhorred
absolute
affection
alas
amazement
ambition
attentive
beheld
beseech
blemish
bountiful
bowsprit
brine
carcass
chanticleer
charity
claps
cloven
companions
confine
conscience
coral
desperation
dispersed
distinctly
divine
dukedom
entrails
fathoms
garment
govern
grudge
grumblings
hag
henchman
hesitate
honeycomb
humble
inclined
infect
knell
lodged
mariners
mortal
nymph
perished
pity
pluck
prime
Providence
reality
request
rigged
sighing
souls
stowed
strive
syllable
tackle
tempest
toil
torment
tortoise
tribute
twixt
ungrateful
unto
usurp
volumes
whelp
withered
yards

Scene 3

bellowing
conspiracy
cram
distinctly
drenched
drowsiness
excel
ghastly
heir
imagination
lack
lush
pierce
porridge
possesses
precedent
preservation
repose
supplant

Scene 4

- acquaints
- assure
- brewing
- celestial
- credulous
- curse
- detract
- fertile
- foul
- hedgehogs
- inherit
- instruct
- keg
- lesser
- marmoset
- nimble
- opinion
- plague
- queasy
- snare
- torment
- trifle
- tyrant

Scene 5

- bashfulness
- odious
- peerless
- perform
- prattle
- precious
- trifling
- unworthiness

Scene 6

- accomplished
- beest
- bid
- civil
- consider
- cunning
- debts
- defy
- doomed
- flout
- harken
- hath
- indignity
- instruments
- jesting
- mocks
- monstrous
- naught
- proceed
- scurvy
- sober
- sorcerer
- twangling
- viceroys
- wilt
- wits

Scene 7

- attend
- banquet
- bedded
- bereft
- deed
- desolate
- desperate
- elements
- exposed
- invulnerable
- legions
- lingering
- opportunity
- perdition
- phoenix
- pronounce
- provoke
- purpose
- tempered
- unicorns
- vigilance

Scene 8

- abjure
- acknowledge
- amazement
- assurance
- auspicious
- bait
- bedimmed
- beheld
- bough
- brace
- briers
- cease
- certain
- chick
- chiefly
- confederates
- conspiracy
- cowslips
- dismayed
- displeasure
- dissolve
- distempered
- distracted
- embrace
- entreat
- expeditious

fabric
fares
fathoms
fetch
foreheads
foretold
gales
hatches
indignation
infect
infinite
inhabits
insubstantial
justify
measured
mischief
mourning
mutinous
nuptial
pageant
paradise
particulars
passion
plot
plummet
preserver
project
promontory
prophesied
pulse
reeling
repose
restore
retain
revels
tabor
thine
thrice
traitors
tread
trod
unnatural
varlets
vexations
vexed
villainous
vision
wardrobe

Characters

Alonzo, King of Naples
Sebastian, his brother
Prospero, Duke of Milan in exile
Antonio, his brother, the usurping Duke of Milan
Ferdinand, son of the King of Naples
Gonzalo, an old councillor
Adrian, a lord
Caliban, slave to Prospero
Trinculo, servant
Stephano, servant
Miranda, daughter of Prospero
Ariel, a spirit

Master of the ship
Boatswain
Mariners
Spirits

The Tempest

Scene 1: A Ship at Sea During a Fierce Storm
(Enter ship's Master and Boatswain.)

Master: Boatswain!

Boatswain: Here, master. What cheer?

Master: Speak to the mariners. Fall to it, or we run ourselves aground! Hurry! Hurry!

(Master exits.)

Boatswain: Hey, you sailors, heave ho! Take in the topsail. Tend to the master's whistle. Wind blow till you must.

(Enter Alonzo, Sebastian, Antonio, Ferdinand, and Gonzalo.)

Alonzo: Good boatswain, do something. Where's the master? Make the men work!

Boatswain: I pray now, keep below.

Antonio: Where is the master, boatswain?

Boatswain: Do you not hear him? You interfere with our work. Keep to your cabins. You do assist the storm.

Gonzalo: Silence!

Boatswain: I will when the sea is! Get out of my way! What cares the storm for the name of a king? To your cabin? Trouble us not.

(Exit Alonzo and Sebastian.)

Gonzalo: You had better remember whom you have aboard!

Boatswain: None that I more love than myself. If you can command these waves to silence, we will not pull a rope more. Use your authority. If you cannot, give thanks you have lived so long and make yourself ready in your cabin for the worst, if it so happen. Heave ho, you sailors. (To Gonzalo) Out of my way, I say!

(Boatswain exits.)

Gonzalo: I have great comfort from this fellow. Methinks he hath no drowning mark upon him. He was born to be hanged!

(Re-enter Boatswain.)

Boatswain: Down with the topmast. Lower! Lower! (To Sebastian and Antonio.) Yet again? What do you here? Shall we give up and drown? Have you a mind to sink?

Sebastian: A pox on your throat you bawling, incharitable dog!

Boatswain: Work you, then!

Antonio: Hang, cur, hang, you insolent noisemaker! We are less afraid to be drowned than thou art.

Gonzalo: Stand fast, good fate, to his hanging. If he be not born to be hanged, our case is miserable.

(Enter mariners.)

Boatswain: Set her two courses off to sea again.

Mariners: All is lost! To prayers, to prayers! All is lost!

Boatswain: Must we drown like rats?

Gonzalo: The King and Prince are at prayers. Let's join them, for our fate is the same as theirs.

Sebastian: I'm out of patience.

Antonio: We are merely cheated of our lives by drunkards. This big mouthed rascal . . . would thou mightest drown!

(Antonio exits.)

Gonzalo: He'll be hanged yet. (Noise and cries off stage.) Mercy on us! We split, we split! Farewell, my wife and children! Farewell brother! We split! We split! We split!

Sebastian: Let's all sink with the King.

(Sebastian exits.)

Gonzalo: Now would I give a thousand miles of sea for an acre of barren ground. The wills above be done, but I wish I could die a dry death!

Scene 2: Prospero's Magical Island a Few Minutes Later
(Enter Miranda and Prospero.)

Miranda: If by your magic, my dearest father, you have caused this storm, please quiet the waters. O, I have suffered with those that I saw suffer. A brave vessel, who had no doubt some noble creatures in her, dashed all to pieces. Poor souls, they perished! Had I any power, I would have sunk the sea within the earth before it could have swallowed the good ship and the frightened souls within her.

Prospero: Collect yourself. Tell your piteous heart there's no harm done.

Miranda: Really, father?

Prospero: No harm. I have done nothing but for thy sake. My dear daughter, who knows not what thou art nor that I am more than just Prospero, master of a poor island.

Miranda: More to know did never enter my thoughts.

Prospero: 'Tis time I should tell thee more. Lend thy hand and pluck my magic garment from me. (Takes off his cape.) Lie there, my art. Wipe your eyes, have comfort. The wreck, which touched thy pity, I have by magic so safely ordered that there is not a soul harmed in the vessel which thou saw'st sink. Sit down, for thou must know further.

Miranda: You have often begun to tell me what I am, but stopped and said "No, not yet."

Prospero: The time has come. Listen and be attentive. Canst thou remember a time before we came unto this island? I do not think thou canst, for then thou wast only three years old.

Miranda: Certainly, sir, I can.

Prospero: What do you remember?

Miranda: 'Tis vague, and more like a dream than reality. Had I not four or five women once that attended me?

Prospero: You did, and more, Miranda. But how is it that this lives in thy mind? What else do you remember? Do you remember how you came here?

Miranda: No, that I do not remember.

Prospero: Twelve years ago, Miranda, thy father was the Duke of Milan and a prince of power.

Miranda: Sir, are you not my father?

Prospero: Yes, I am your father and I was Duke of Milan, and my only daughter a princess no less.

Miranda: I was a princess? What foul play had we that we came from Milan to this? Or was it a good thing?

Prospero: Both, both my daughter. By foul play we were heaved into the sea but blessedly drifted to this island.

Miranda: O, my heart bleeds to think of the trouble that I have been to you. Please go on.

Prospero: You have an uncle named Antonio, my brother. O that a brother should be so wicked! Well, I let him govern in my place so that I could study my books. Are you listening to me?

Miranda: O yes, sir.

Prospero: Well, your wicked uncle took advantage of my desire to better my mind and began to whisper that he would make a better ruler than I. You are not paying attention.

Miranda: O good father, I am. Most heedfully.

Prospero: Now mark this. While I was studying these great books of magic, my ungrateful brother began to wish for more power and yet more power. He wanted to be the royal duke himself, with absolute power. Do you hear me?

Miranda: Your tale, sir, would cure deafness.

Prospero: My library was dukedom large enough for me. Finally, your uncle Antonio went to the King of Naples. Now this King of Naples was an enemy of mine for a long time. Antonio promised the king to pay him twice the tribute in taxes that I had paid, if the King would usurp my dukedom and give it over unto him, my brother. The King agreed, and then one midnight Antonio and his henchman abducted me and my crying child . . . you . . . yourself!

Miranda: Why did not they that hour destroy us?

Prospero: Well you might ask. Dear child, they did not dare for I was too well loved by the people, but they hurried us aboard a ship in the dead of darkness and took us out to sea. There they put us into a rotten carcass of a boat, not rigged, nor tackle, nor sail, nor mast. The very rats had deserted it! There they left us to the mercy of the storm.

Miranda: O dear father, what trouble I must have been!

Prospero: No, you were a little angel that did save me from going mad. You did smile, which raised in me a hope to bear up under it all.

Miranda: How came we ashore?

Prospero: By divine Providence. Some food we had and some fresh water that a nobleman, Gonzalo, out of his charity did give us with rich garments, stuffs, and necessaries which since have saved our lives. And out of his kindness, knowing I loved my books, he furnished me from my own library with volumes that I prize above my dukedom.

Miranda: I wish I could see that man named Gonzalo.

Prospero: Now I arise. Sit still and hear the last of our sea sorrow. Here in this island we arrived and here have I, thy schoolmaster, taught thee more than other princesses know that have tutors not so careful.

Miranda: Heavens thank you for it. And now, I pray you sir, for still 'tis beating in my mind, your reason for raising this sea storm?

Prospero: I'll tell you this much. By accident most strange, bountiful fortune hath brought mine enemies to this very shore. And by my magic here's my opportunity. If I don't take it, my fortune will ever after droop. Cease with questions. Thou art inclined to sleep. You have no choice. (Miranda falls asleep.) Come to me, servant, come. I am ready now. Approach, my Ariel. Come!

(Enter Ariel.)

Ariel: All hail, great master, good sir, hail! I come to answer thy best pleasure, be it to fly, to swim, to dive into fire, to ride on curled clouds, to thy strong bidding command Ariel.

Prospero: Hast thou, spirit, caused the tempest that I ordered?

Ariel: To the last detail. I boarded the king's ship. Now on the beak, now in the waist, the deck, in every cabin I flamed amazement. Sometimes I'd divide and burn in many places. On the topmast, the yards and bowsprit would I flame distinctly, then meet and join. Lightning and thunder claps were not more frightening.

Prospero: My spirit, who was so brave that this experience would not infect his reason?

Ariel: Not a soul. Everyone felt a fever of the mad and played some tricks of desperation. All but the mariners plunged in the foaming brine and quit the vessel. The king's son, Ferdinand, with hair standing on end was the first man that leapt.

Prospero: But was this near the shore?

Ariel: Close by, my master.

Prospero: But are they safe, Ariel?

Ariel: Not a hair perished. On their garments not a blemish, but fresher than before. And as you ordered, I have dispersed them in groups about the island. The king's son have I landed by himself whom I left sighing and sitting, his arms folded thus.

Prospero: What did you do with the ship, the mariners, and all the rest of the fleet?

Ariel: The king's ship is safely in the bay, in the deep nook she's hid. The mariners are all under hatches stowed, fast asleep. And for the rest of the fleet, they all are upon the Mediterranean bound safely for home, for Naples, thinking they saw the king's ship wrecked and the king drowned.

Prospero: Ariel, thy work was well performed, but there's more work. What is the time of the day?

Ariel: Past noon.

Prospero: At least two hours. The time 'twixt six and now by us be spent most preciously.

Ariel: Is there more toil? Remember what thou hast promised, which is not yet performed me?

Prospero: How now? What is it thou canst command?

Ariel: My liberty!

Prospero: What! Before time be out? No indeed!

Ariel: I beg you! Remember I have done thee worthy service told thee no lies, made no mistakes, served without grudge or grumblings. Thou didst promise to free me a full year ago.

Prospero: Dost thou forget from what a torment I did free thee?

Ariel: No, I do not, sir.

Prospero: Thou liest! Hast thou forgot the foul Sycorax? Hast thou forgot her?

Ariel: No, sir.

Prospero: This wicked woman was hither brought with her child, and here was left by the sailors. Thou wast then her servant and you were a spirit too delicate to act her earthy and abhorred commands, so she did confine thee by her magic into a cloven pine where imprisoned thou didst painfully remain a dozen years. She died and left thee there. Then was this island saved for the son that she did bring here, a freckled whelp hag-born, not honoured with a human shape.

Ariel: Yes, Caliban her son.

Prospero: Dull thing he, that Caliban whom now I keep in service. Thou best knowest what torment I did find thee in. It was a torment which Sycorax herself could not again undo. It was mine art that made the pine tree open and let thee out.

Ariel: I thank thee, master.

Prospero: If you continue to complain, I will put thee in the knotty entrails of an oak till thou howlest away twelve winters.

Ariel: Pardon, master. I will obey your commands.

Prospero: Do so. And after two days I will give you your freedom

Ariel: My noble master! What shall I do? Say!

Prospero: Go make thyself like a nymph over the sea. Be invisible to every eyeball but mine. Go take this shape, and then come to me. Go! (Exit Ariel. Turning to Miranda.) Awake, dear heart, awake! Thou hast slept well. Awake!

Miranda: The strangeness of your story put me to sleep.

Prospero: Come. We'll visit Caliban, my slave, who never gives us kind answer.

Miranda: 'Tis a villain, sir, I do not love to look on.

Prospero: But we must! He makes our fire, fetches in our wood, and serves us well. What ho! Slave! Caliban! You piece of earth, speak!

Caliban: (From within a deep hole.)
I've brought in wood enough.

Prospero: Come forth I say. There's other business for you. Come, you tortoise. (Re-enter Ariel.) My quaint Ariel, let me whisper in your ear.

Ariel: My lord, it shall be done.

(Ariel exits.)

Prospero: Thou poisonous slave, come forth.

(Enter Caliban.)

Caliban: A curse on you! Both of you!

Prospero: For this, tonight you shall have cramps. Thou shall be pinched by spirits as thick as honeycomb, each pinch more stinging than bees that made them.

Caliban: I must eat my dinner. This island's mine, by Sycorax, my mother, which you took away from me. You used to stroke me and make much of me. You would give me water with berries in it and teach me how to name the big stars. Then I loved you and showed you all the island, the fresh springs and fertile places. Cursed be that I did so. May all the charms of Sycorax, toads, beetles, bats light on you! For I am all the subjects that you have. I was my own king. And here you keep me in this cave and won't let me roam the rest of the island.

Prospero: Lying slave! I was kind to you and lodged you in my own cell till you frightened Miranda with your curses.

Caliban: I hate her!

Miranda: Why Caliban, I pitied thee, took pains to teach you to speak, taught you each hour one thing to another.

Caliban: You taught me language, and my profit is I know how to curse. I curse you for teaching me.

Prospero: Brute, be gone. Fetch us in fuel and be quick about it. You hesitate? If you neglect or do unwillingly what I command, I'll make you roar that beasts shall tremble at your yelling.

Caliban: No, please! (Aside.) I must obey, his art is too powerful.

Prospero: So, slave go!

(Exit Caliban. Enter Ferdinand and Ariel. Ariel is invisible.)

Ariel: (Singing.)
Come unto these yellow sands,
And then take hands,
Hark, hark, the watchdogs bark.
Hark, hark I hear
The strain of a strutting chanticleer.

Ferdinand: Where is the music coming from, the air or the earth? It sounds no more. Sitting on a bank weeping for the King my father's death, this magic crept by me upon the waters and I have followed it here. But 'tis gone. No, it begins again.

Ariel: (Singing.)
Full fathoms five thy father lies,
Of his bones are coral made.
Those are pearls that were his eyes,
Nothing of him that doth fade
But doth suffer a sea change
Into something rich and strange.
Sea nymphs hourly ring his knell.
Hark now, I hear them—Ding, dong bell.

Ferdinand: The song is about my drowned father. This is no mortal business, nor no natural sound. I hear it now above me.

Prospero: Look, Miranda, tell me what you see yonder.

Miranda: What is it? A spirit? How it looks about. It carries a brave form. But it is a spirit!

Prospero: No, child, it eats and sleeps as we do. This boy which you see was in the wreck. He has lost his companions and strays about to find them.

Miranda: I might call him a thing divine, for nothing natural I ever saw so handsome!

Prospero: (Aside.)
It goes, I see, as I wish. Spirit Ariel, fine spirit, I'll free thee within two days for this.

Ferdinand: (Seeing Miranda.)
That must be the goddess of these songs. May I please know if you live on this island, and will you tell me where I am? My prime request is if you be real or a vision?

Miranda: But certainly, I am real.

Ferdinand: She speaks my language? Heavens, I am the best of them that speaks this speech, were I but where 'tis spoken.

Prospero: The best? What if the King of Naples heard thee?

Ferdinand: He does hear me, and that he does I weep. I am now King of Naples, who with my own eyes beheld the king my father drowned.

Miranda: Alas!

Ferdinand: Yes, and all his lords.

Prospero: (Aside.)
At the first sight they have fallen in love. Delicate Ariel, I'll set thee free for this. Quiet, sir. Be quiet!

Miranda: Why speaks my father so urgently? This is the third man that ever I saw, the first that ever I sighed for. Pity, move my father to be inclined my way.

Ferdinand: If you're not already married and your affection not gone forth, I'll make you the Queen of Naples.

Prospero: (Aside.)
They are both in each others' powers, but I must make it difficult, lest too light winning make the prize light. (To Ferdinand.) One word, I charge you to listen to me. You are not the King of Naples, but a spy and have come to take this island from me.

Ferdinand: No, as I am a man.

Miranda: There's nothing ill can dwell in such a temple. If the ill spirit have so fair a house, good things will strive to swell within it.

Prospero: Follow me. Speak you not for him. He's a traitor. Come, I'll manacle your neck and feet together. Follow! Sea water shalt thou drink. Thy food shalt be withered roots.

Ferdinand: No! I will resist!

(Draws his sword but is frozen under a spell by Prospero.)

Miranda: O dear father, don't treat him badly.

Prospero: Put your sword up, traitor. You make a show but dare not strike, your conscience is so guilty. I can disarm you with this stick and make your weapon drop.

Miranda: I beseech you, father.

Prospero: Hang not on my garments.

Miranda: Sir, have pity, I'll vouch for his good conduct.

Prospero: Silence. Not one word more! You think there are no more such shapes as he, having seen but him and Caliban. Foolish girl!

Miranda: My affections are, then, most humble. I have no ambition to see a goodlier man.

Prospero: Come on, obey. I have paralyzed you with my magic.

Ferdinand: I can't move! But your threats are nothing to me, if I can but through my prison once a day behold this maid.

Prospero: (Aside.)
It works. (To Ferdinand.) Come. (To Ariel.) You have done well, fine Ariel.

Miranda: Be of comfort, my father's of a better nature than he appears by speech. He is usually very kind.

Prospero: (To Ariel.)
You shall be as free as mountain winds, but then you must do exactly as I command you.

Ariel: To the syllable.

Prospero: Come follow. Speak not for him.

Scene 3: Another Part of the Island
(Enter Gonzalo, Alonzo, Sebastian, Antonio, Adrian, and others.)

Gonzalo: I beseech you, sir, be merry. You have cause for joy. So have we all, for our escape is a miracle. I mean our preservation. Few in millions can speak like us. Then wisely, good sir, weigh our sorrow with our comfort.

Alonzo: I pray you, be quiet.

Sebastian: He receives comfort like cold porridge.

Antonio: Look, he's winding up his brain like a watch.

Adrian: The air breathes upon us here most sweetly.

Sebastian: As if it had lungs, and rotten ones.

Antonio: Or as if it were perfumed by a swamp.

Gonzalo: Here is everything advantageous to life.

Antonio: True, save means to live.

Sebastian: Of that there's none or little.

Gonzalo: How lush and green the grass looks. Our garments, despite being drenched in the sea, are now as fresh as when we put them on first in Africa, at the marriage of the king's fair daughter Claribel to the King of Tunis.

Alonzo: You cram these words into mine ears. Would I had never married my daughter there! My son is lost. I shall never see my daughter again. O my son, what strange fish hath made his meal on thee?

Adrian:	Sir, he may live. I saw him swimming. His bold head above the waves he kept and oared himself with his good arms in lusty strokes to the shore. I doubt not he came alive to land.
Alonzo:	No, no. He's gone.
Sebastian:	We kneeled to you and begged you not to take this trip. You have lost your son, I fear, forever. The fault's your own.
Alonzo:	So is the loss.
Gonzalo:	My lord Sebastian, the truth you speak doth lack some gentleness. You rub the sore when you should bring the medicine. (To the king.) It is foul weather in us all, good sir, when you are cloudy.
Antonio:	Very foul.
Gonzalo:	If I were king of this isle, I would govern with such perfection to excel the golden age.
Antonio:	Long live Gonzalo.
Gonzalo:	And mark me, sir, if . . .
Alonzo:	Prithee, no more. Thou dost talk nonsense.
Gonzalo:	I do, your highness, and did it to entertain these gentle men who always laugh at nonsense.
Antonio:	'Twas you we laughed at.
	(Enter Ariel.)
Sebastian:	Nay, my good lord, be not angry.
Gonzalo:	No, you're too important to me. Will you laugh me asleep, for I am very heavy?
Antonio:	Go to sleep then.
	(Ariel puts everyone to sleep except Alonzo, Sebastian, and Antonio.)

Alonzo: What, so soon asleep? I wish mine eyes would shut out my thoughts.

Antonio: We two, my lord, will guard your person while you take your rest and watch your safety.

(Alonzo sleeps. Exit Ariel.)

Sebastian: What a strange drowsiness possesses them.

Antonio: It is the quality of the climate.

Sebastian: Why does it not then make us sleep?

Antonio: I'm wide awake. They fell asleep as if by a thunder stroke. What might, worthy Sebastian? O, what might? No more . . . And yet methinks I see it in thy face what thou shouldst be. My strong imagination sees a crown dropping upon thy head.

Sebastian: What art thou awake?

Antonio: Do you not hear me speak?

Sebastian: I do, and surely it is a sleepy language and thou speakest out of thy sleep. What didst thou say?

Antonio: Noble Sebastian, thou let'st thy fortune sleep. Die, rather while thou art waking.

Sebastian: Thou dost snore distinctly. There's meaning in thy snores.

Antonio: Oh, if you but knew!

Sebastian: Prithee, say on.

Antonio: Thus, sir. (Points to Gonzalo.) Although this lord, this old fool, almost persuaded the King his son's alive, that's impossible.

Sebastian: I have no hope that he's still alive.

Antonio: Out of that "no hope," what great hope have you? No hope that way is another way so high a hope that even ambition cannot pierce a wink beyond, but doubt discovery there. Will you grant with me that Ferdinand is drowned?

Sebastian: Yes, he's dead.

Antonio: Then, tell me, who's the next heir to the throne?

Sebastian: Claribel.

Antonio: She that is Queen of Tunis? She that dwells halfway round the world? What's past is past. What is to come is up to you and me.

Sebastian: What stuff is this? How say you? 'Tis true, my brother's daughter is Queen of Tunis, but so is she heir to the throne of Naples 'twixt which regions there is great distance.

Antonio: A distance whose every mile seems to cry out, "How shall that Claribel get back to Naples? Keep in Tunis and let Sebastian wake!" Let's say this were death that now hath seized them. Why they were no worse than now they are. There can be those that can rule Naples as well as he that sleeps and lords that can speak nonsense as well as this Gonzalo. O, that you bore that mind that I do. What a chance were this for your advancement. Do you under stand me?

Sebastian: Methinks I do. I remember you did supplant your brother Prospero.

Antonio: True, and look how well my garments sit upon me, much better than before. My brother's servants were then my equals. Now they are my servants.

Sebastian: But for your conscience . . .

Antonio: Conscience? Where lies that? I have no conscience. Twenty consciences could not stand 'twixt me and such power. Here lies your brother, no better than the earth he lies upon, as if he were dead, whom I, with three inches of steel, can put to sleep forever, while you the same to Gonzalo. For all the rest, they'll take suggestion as a cat laps milk.

Sebastian: Your example, dear friend, shall be my precedent. As you got your dukedom, I'll get my crown. Draw thy sword. One stroke shall free thee from the tribute which thou payest, and I the new king shall love thee.

Antonio: Draw together. When I rear my hand, do you the like to fall it on Gonzalo.

Sebastian: O, but one word.

(Enter Ariel.)

Ariel: My master through his magic art foresees the danger that you, his friend, are in and sends me forth to keep them living.
(Sings in Gonzalo's ear.)
While you here do snoring lie,
Open-eyed conspiracy
His time doth take.
If of a life you keep a care,
Shake off slumber and beware,
Awake, awake!

Antonio: Then let us both be sudden.

Gonzalo: (Awakes.)
Why, how now? Alonzo, awake! Why are your swords drawn? Wherefore these ghastly faces?

Alonzo: What's the matter?

Sebastian: While we stood here securing your repose, even now we heard a burst of bellowing like bulls, or rather lions. Did it not wake you? It was terrible.

Alonzo: I heard nothing.

Antonio: O 'twas a din to fright a monster's ears, to make an earthquake! Sure it was the roar of a whole herd of lions.

Alonzo: Heard you this, Gonzalo?

Gonzalo: Upon mine honour, sir, I heard a humming, and that a strange one too, which did awake me. I shaked you, sir, and cried. As mine eyes opened I saw their weapons drawn. There was a noise, that's true. 'Tis best we stand upon our guard or that we leave this place. Let's draw our weapons.

Alonzo: Yes, let's leave here, and let's make further search for my poor son.

Gonzalo: Heavens keep him from these beasts, for he is surely on the island.

Alonzo: Lead away.

Ariel: Prospero, my lord, shall know what I have done. So king, go safely on to seek your son.

Scene 4: Another Part of the Island

(Enter Caliban.)

Caliban: A curse on Prospero! His spirits hear me, and yet I must curse him. But they will not torment me, unless he bid them. Yet for every trifle are they set upon me, sometimes like apes that chatter at me and after bite me, then like hedgehogs, which lie tumbling in my barefoot way and stick my feet. (Enter Trinculo.) Lo, now, here comes a spirit of his and to torment me for bringing wood in slowly. I'll fall flat, maybe he will not see me.

Trinculo: Here's not a bush nor a shrub to keep off the weather. And another storm brewing. If it should thunder as it did before, I don't know where to hide my head. What have we here? A man or fish? Dead or alive? A fish, he smells like a fish. A very old and fish-like smell. A strange fish. He has legs like a man, and his fins are arms. In my opinion, this is no fish, but an islander that has been struck by a thunderbolt. (Thunder is heard.) Alas, the storm is come again. I'd better creep under his cape. There is no other shelter hereabout. Misery acquaints a man with strange bedfellows. I will stay under here till the storm is over.

(Trinculo creeps under Caliban's cape. Enter Stephano, singing.)

Stephano: I shall no more to sea, to sea . . . here I shall die ashore.

Caliban: (From under his cape.)
Do not torment me!

Stephano: What's the matter? Huh? I have not escaped drowning to be afraid now of your four legs.

Caliban: The spirit torments me! O!

Stephano: This is some monster of the isle with four legs who has got the measles. Where should he learn our language? I will give him some relief.

Caliban: Do not torment me, please. I'll bring my wood home faster.

Stephano: He's having a fit now, and does not talk after the wisest. If I can tame him, he'll make a good house pet.

Trinculo: (Under cape.)
I know that voice. It should be . . . but he is drowned, and these are spirits. O defend me!

Stephano: Four legs and two voices . . . a most unusual monster. His forward voice is to speak well of his friend, but his backward voice is to utter foul speeches to detract. If a sip of wine will recover him, I will cure his fever. Come, I will pour some in his other mouth.

Trinculo: Stephano!

Stephano: Does your other mouth call me? Mercy! Mercy! This is a devil and no monster. I will leave him.

(Starts to run away.)

Trinculo: Stephano! If you are Stephano, touch me and speak to me. For I am Trinculo . . . don't be afraid . . . your good friend, Trinculo.

Stephano: If you are Trinculo, come forth. I'll pull you by the lesser legs. If any be Trinculo's legs, these are they. (Draws Trinculo out by the legs.) It is Trinculo! How did you come to be joined to this moon calf?

Trinculo: I took him to be killed with a thunder stroke. But you are not drowned, Stephano? I hope now you are not drowned. Is the storm over? I hid under the dead moon calf's cape for fear of the storm. And are you living Stephano? O Stephano, two Neapolitans escaped.

Stephano: Please do not turn me about. My stomach is a little queasy.

Caliban: That's a brave god. I will kneel to him.

Stephano: How did you escape? How did you get here? I escaped upon a keg of wine which the sailors heaved overboard. This bottle I made of the bark of a tree with my own hands.

Caliban: I'll swear upon that bottle to be your true subject, for the drink is not earthly.

Stephano: Here. Swear then. How did you escape?

Trinculo: Swam ashore, man, like a duck. I can swim like a duck.

Stephano: Though you can swim like a duck, you are a goose.

Trinculo: O Stephano, have you anymore of this wine?

Stephano: The whole barrel, man, my cellar is in a rock by the seaside where the wine is hid. How now, moon calf, how do you feel now?

Caliban: Have you dropped from heaven?

Stephano: Ay, out of the moon, I assure you. I used to be the man in the moon.

Caliban: I have seen thee in her. And I do adore thee. My mistress showed you to me.

Trinculo: This is a very stupid monster. I'm afraid of him. A very dumb monster. The man in the moon? A most poor credulous monster.

Caliban: I'll show you every fertile inch of the island, and I will kiss your foot. Please, be my god.

Trinculo: A crazy monster!

Caliban: I'll kiss thy foot. I'll swear myself your subject.

Stephano: Come on then. Down and swear.

Trinculo: I shall laugh myself to death at this puppy-headed monster. He's so foolish.

Stephano: Come, kiss.

Trinculo: The poor monster's mad.

Caliban: I'll show thee the best springs. I'll pluck berries for thee. I'll fish for thee and get good wood for thee. A plague upon the tyrant that I serve. I'll serve him no more but follow thee, thou wondrous man.

Trinculo: A most ridiculous monster to make a wonder of a poor man.

Caliban: I prithee, let me bring thee where crabs grow, and I with my long nails will dig thee pig nuts, show thee a jay's nest, and instruct thee how to snare the nimble marmoset. Wilt thou go?

Stephano: I prithee now, lead the way without any more talking. Trinculo, the king and all our company else being drowned, we will inherit here. Here bear my bottle, fellow. Trinculo, we'll fill him by and by again.

Caliban: (Singing.)
Farewell, master. Farewell, master!

Trinculo: A howling monster . . . an absurd monster!

Caliban: No more dams I'll make for fish,
Nor ever wash another dish.
Bab-ban Ca-Caliban
Has a new master—get a new man.
Freedom! Freedom! Freedom!

Stephano: O brave monster, lead the way.

(All exit.)

Scene 5: Prospero's Part of the Island an Hour Later
(Enter Ferdinand carrying a log.)

Ferdinand: This task would be odious to me, but for the mistress which I serve. She makes my work pleasant. O, she is ten times more gentle than her father. I must remove some thousands of these logs and pile them up just to please him. My sweet mistress weeps when she sees me work.

(Enter Miranda, with Prospero following several steps behind.)

Miranda: Alas, now pray you, work not so hard. I would the lightning had burnt up those logs. Pray, set it down and rest. When this burns 'twill weep for having wearied you. My father is hard at study. Pray now, rest yourself.

Ferdinand: Dear mistress, the sun will set before I finish my work.

Miranda: If you sit down, I'll bear your logs the while. Pray, give me that, I'll carry it to the pile.

Ferdinand: No, precious creature, I had rather break my back than let you do such work as this.

Miranda: It would become me as well as it does you, and I should do it with much more ease, for my good will is to it and yours it is against.

Prospero: (Aside.)
Poor boy, you are caught . . . ha-ha!

Miranda: You look tired.

Ferdinand: No, noble mistress, 'tis fresh morning with me when you are around. Please tell me your name.

Miranda: Miranda. O, my father, I have broke my promise to tell you.

Ferdinand: Admired Miranda! Many a lady I have eyed with best regard, and I have liked several women, but each of them had some defect. But you, oh you, so perfect and so peerless, are created of every woman's best.

Miranda: I do not know one of my sex, no woman's face remember, save mine own. Nor have I seen more that I may call men than you, good friend, and my dear father. But I would not wish any companion in the world but you. But I prattle too wildly and do forget my promise to my father.

Ferdinand: I am a prince, Miranda. I do think, a king, I would not so. Hear my soul speak. The very instant I saw you, I fell in love with you.

Miranda: Do you love me?

Ferdinand: O heaven, O earth, bear witness to this sound. I, beyond all limit of what else in the world do love, prize, honour you.

Miranda: I am a fool to weep at what I am glad of.

Prospero: (Aside.)
May heavens rain grace on them.

Ferdinand: Why are you weeping?

Miranda: At mine unworthiness. But this is trifling, away bashfulness. I am your wife, if you will marry me. If not, I'll die your servant whether you will or no.

Ferdinand: My mistress dearest.

Miranda: My husband then?

Ferdinand: Ay, with a willing heart. Here's my hand.

Miranda: And mine with my heart in it.

(Exit Ferdinand and Miranda.)

Prospero: Well, that's that. Now I must go to my book of magic. Before supper time I have much business to perform.

Scene 6: Another Part of the Island
(Enter Sebastian, Trinculo, and Caliban.)

Stephano: Don't tell me. When the barrel is empty we will drink water, not a drop before. Therefore, servant monster, drink to me.

Trinculo: Servant monster? O me! They say there's but five upon this isle. We are three of them. If the other two be brained like us, the island is doomed.

Stephano: Drink, servant monster, when I bid thee. Thy eyes are almost set in thy head.

Trinculo: Where else should they be set? He would be a brave monster indeed, if they were set in his tail.

Stephano: My man-monster hath drowned his tongue in wine. Moon calf speak, if thou beest a good moon calf.

Caliban: Let me lick thy shoe. I'll not serve him, he is drunk.

Trinculo: Thou liest, ignorant monster, I am as sober as a judge. Wilt thou tell a monstrous lie, being but half a fish and half a monster?

Caliban: Hear how he mocks me? Wilt thou let him, my lord?

Trinculo: "Lord" quoth he. That a monster should be such a fool!

Caliban: Lo, lo, again. Bite him to death, I prithee.

Stephano: Trinculo, keep a civil tongue in your head. The poor monster's my subject, and he shall not suffer indignity.

Caliban: I thank my noble lord. Wilt thou be pleased to harken once again to the suit I made to thee?

Stephano: Yes. Kneel and repeat it! I will stand, and so shall Trinculo.

(Enter Ariel, invisible.)

Caliban: As I told thee before, I am subject to a tyrant, a sorcerer, that by his cunning hath cheated me of the island.

Ariel: Thou liest.

Caliban: (To Trinculo.)
Thou liest, thou jesting monkey. I would my valiant master would destroy thee. I do not lie.

Stephano: Trinculo, if you trouble him any more, so help me I will supplant some of your teeth.

Trinculo: Why, I said nothing.

Stephano: Mum then, and no more. Proceed.

Caliban: I say, by sorcery he got this island from me. Thy greatness will revenge me, for I know thou darest, but this thing dare not.

Stephano: That's most certain.

Caliban: Thou shalt be lord of it, and I'll serve thee.

Stephano: How now shall this be accomplished. Can you bring me to the party?

Caliban: Yes, my lord, while he's asleep, where thou mayst knock him in the head.

Ariel: Thou liest, thou canst not!

Caliban: Thou scurvy patch! I do beseech thy greatness, give him blows and take his bottle from him. When that's gone, he shall drink naught but brine, for I'll not show him where the fresh water is.

Stephano: Trinculo, interrupt the monster once more, and by this hand I'll turn my mercy out of doors and make mincemeat of thee.

Trinculo: What did I do? I did nothing. I'll go further off.

Stephano: Did you not say he lied?

Ariel: Thou liest.

Stephano: Do I? Take that! (Strikes Trinculo.) Go ahead, lie again!

Trinculo: I did not lie. Are you out of your wits and hearing too?

Caliban: Ha-ha-ha!

Stephano: Now, forward with your tale. Trinculo, stand further off.

Caliban: Strike him! After a little I'll strike him too.

Stephano: Come, proceed.

Caliban: Why, as I told thee, 'tis a custom with him in the afternoon to sleep. Then, thou mayst brain him, having first seized his books. Remember first to possess his books, for without them he's but a sot, nor hath not one spirit to command. Burn but his books. And then most deeply to consider is the beauty of his daughter.

Stephano: His daughter? Pretty, eh?

Caliban: Ay, my lord. She will make a good queen.

Stephano: All right, monster, I will kill this man. His daughter and I will be king and queen, and Trinculo and thyself shall be viceroys. Dost thou like the plot, Trinculo?

Trinculo: Excellent.

Stephano: Give me thy hand. I am sorry I strike thee. But, while thou livest, keep a civil tongue in thy head.

Caliban: Within this half hour he will be asleep. Wilt thou destroy him then?

Stephano: Ay, on mine honour.

Ariel: This will I tell my master.

Caliban: Thou makest me merry. I am full of pleasure. Let us be jocund. Will you sing the song you taught me?

Stephano: At thy request, monster, I will sing it. Come on Trinculo, let us sing.
(Sings.)
Flout them and scout them,
Scout them and flout them,
Thought is free.

Caliban: That's not the tune.

(Ariel plays the tune on an instrument.)

Stephano: What is this?

Trinculo: This is the tune of our song played by the picture of nobody.

Stephano: If thou beest a man, show thyself in thy likeness. If thou beest a spirit . . .

Trinculo: O, forgive me my sins.

Stephano: He that dies pays all debts. I defy thee. Mercy on us!

Caliban: Art thou afraid?

Stephano: No, monster, not I.

Caliban: Be not afraid, the island is full of noises, sounds, and sweet airs that give delight and hurt not. Sometimes a thousand twanging instruments will hum about mine ears. And sometimes voices will make me sleep again, and then, in dreaming, the clouds I thought would open and show riches ready to drop upon me, so that when I waked I cried to dream again.

Stephano: This will prove a brave kingdom to me, where I shall have my music for nothing.

Caliban: When Prospero is destroyed!

Stephano: That shall be by and by. I remember the story.

Trinculo: The sound is going away. Let's follow it and after do our work.

Stephano: Lead, monster, we'll follow. I wish I could see this master. He is a good musician.

Trinculo: I'll follow Stephano.

(All exit.)

Scene 7: Another Part of the Island
(Enter Alonzo, Sebastian, Antonio, Gonzalo, Adrian, and others.)

Gonzalo: O my lord, I can go no further, sir. My old bones ache. By your patience, I must rest.

Alonzo: Old lord, I cannot blame thee. I am tired myself. Sit down and rest. I will put off my hope and keep it no longer. My son is drowned whom thus we stray to find. Well, let him go.

Antonio: (Aside.)
Do not for one minute forget the purpose that you decided upon!

Sebastian: (Aside.)
We'll take the next opportunity.

Antonio: (Aside.)
Let it be tonight for now they are tired. They cannot use such vigilance as when they are fresh.

Sebastian: (Aside.)
All right. Tonight! Now be quiet!

(Enter Prospero, invisible. Music is heard.)

Alonzo: What's that? My good friends, listen!

Gonzalo: Marvellous sweet music.

(Enter strange shapes bringing in a banquet. They dance about and depart.)

Alonzo: Heavens, what were these?

Sebastian: Now I will believe that there are unicorns and that the phoenix does indeed exist.

Antonio: Now I'd believe anything!

Gonzalo: If in Naples I should report this, would they believe me? These must be people of the island. They are of monstrous shape, yet their manners are more gentle almost than any human's.

Prospero: (Aside.)
Honest lord, thou hast said well. For some there are worse than devils. Depart spirits!

Adrian: They vanished strangely.

Sebastian: No matter, since they have left their banquet behind, for we are hungry. (To Alonzo.) Will it please you to taste of what is here?

Alonzo: Not I.

Gonzalo: Faith, sir, you need not fear.

Alonzo: I will feed, although my last. No matter, since I feel the best is past. Brother, my lord the Duke, stand to and do as we.

(Enter Ariel who makes banquet vanish.)

Ariel: You are three men of sin whom destiny has caused to be shipwrecked on this island. You among men being most unfit to live, I have made you mad. (Men draw their swords.) You fools, elements of whom your swords are tempered may as well wound the loud winds as strike at me. I am vulnerable. If you could hurt, your swords are not too heavy for you and will not be uplifted. But re member that you three from Milan did supplant good Prospero! Exposed him and his innocent child unto the sea. For which foul deed you shall pay most dearly! Thee of thy son, Alonzo, are bereft and lingering perdition, worse than any death, shall step by step attend you here in this most desolate island.

(Ariel vanishes. Shapes and shadows remove banquet table.)

Prospero: (Aside.)
Bravely thou hast performed, my Ariel. Of my instruction hast thou nothing left undone. My high charms work, and these mine enemies are now all in my power. And in these fits I leave them, while I visit young Ferdinand whom they suppose is drowned.

(Prospero exits.)

Gonzalo: In the name of something holy, sir, why stand you in this strange stare?

Alonzo: O, it is monstrous, monstrous! I thought the thunder spoke and told me of it. The winds did pronounce the name of Prospero. My son in the ooze is bedded and I'll seek him deeper and with him there lie mudded.

(Alonzo exits.)

Sebastian: But one fiend at a time, I'll fight their legions over.

Antonio: I'll be thy second.

(Exit Sebastian and Antonio.)

Gonzalo: All three of them are desperate. Their great guilt now begins to bite the spirits. I must follow them and hinder them from what this madness may now provoke them to.

Adrian: I'll follow.

Scene 8: Prospero's Tent a Short While Later
(Enter Prospero, Miranda, and Ferdinand.)

Prospero: Ferdinand, all the vexations were but my trials of thy love, and thou hast stood the test. Here, before Heaven, take my daughter for your wife.

Ferdinand: O sir, was ever a man happier?

Prospero: Well spoken. Sit, then, and talk with her. She is thine own.

Ferdinand: Let me live here forever. So rare a father and a wife makes this place paradise.

Prospero: (Aside.)
I had forgot that foul conspiracy of the beast Caliban and his confederates against my life. The minute of their plot is almost come.

Ferdinand: This is strange. Your father's in some passion that works him strongly.

Miranda: Never till this day saw I him touched with anger so distempered.

Prospero: You do look, my son, as if you were dismayed. Sir, I am vexed. Bear with my weakness, my old brain is troubled. Be not disturbed. If you wish, return into my cell and there repose. A turn or two I'll walk to still my beating mind.

Ferdinand: We wish you peace.

(Exit Miranda and Ferdinand.)

Prospero: (To Ariel.)
Come! I thank thee, Ariel. Come!

(Enter Ariel.)

Ariel: Thy thought I cleave to. What's thy pleasure?

Prospero: Spirit, we must prepare to meet Caliban.

Ariel: Ay, my commander, I thought to have told thee of it, but feared I might anger thee.

Prospero: Say again, where didst thou leave these varlets?

Ariel: I told, you sir, they were always bending toward their project. Then I beat my tabor, at which they pricked their ears, advanced their eyelids, lifted up their noses as they smelt music. So I charmed their ears that they followed through toothed briers and thorns which entered their frail shins. At last I left them in the filthy pool beyond your cell, there dancing up to their chins, that the foul lake outstunk their feet.

Prospero: This was well done, my bird. Thy shape invisible retain. The costumes in my house go bring hither for bait to catch these thieves.

Ariel: I go! I go!

(Ariel exits.)

Prospero: I will plague all three, even to roaring. (Re-enter Ariel with an armload of capes and robes.) Come, hang them on this line.

(Enter Caliban, Stephano, and Trinculo all sopping wet.)

Caliban: Pray you, tread softly, that Prospero may not hear a foot fall. We now are near his cell.

Stephano: Monster, your fairy, which you say is a harmless fairy, has played the devil with us.

Trinculo: Monster, I smell like a skunk, at which my nose is in great indignation.

Stephano: So is mine. Do you hear, monster? If I should take displeasure against you, look out . . .

Trinculo: Thou wouldst become a lost monster.

Caliban: My lord, be patient, for the prize I'll bring to thee shall be worth it. Therefore, speak softly.

Trinculo: Ay, but to lose our bottles in the pool!

Stephano: There is not only disgrace and dishonour in that, monster, but an infinite loss.

Caliban: Prithee, my king, be quiet. Seest thou there. This is the mouth of the cell. No noise and enter. Do that good mischief which may make this island thine own forever and I, thy Caliban.

Stephano: Give me thy hand.

Trinculo: (Seeing garments on the line.)
O King Stephano! O worthy Stephano! Look what wardrobe here is for thee!

Caliban: Let it alone, thou fool, it is but trash.

Trinculo: O ho, monster, we know what is trash and what is not! O King Stephano!

Stephano: Take off that robe. Trinculo, give me that robe!

Trinculo: Thy grace shall have it.

Caliban: Let it alone, and do the deed first. If he awake, he'll fill our skins with pinches and make us strange stuff.

Stephano: Be you quiet, monster! (To Trinculo.) Here's a garment for you. You shall not go unrewarded while I am king of this country. There's another garment for you.

Trinculo: Monster, come and help us pack up the rest.

Caliban: I will have none of it. We shall lose our time and all be turned to apes with foreheads villainous low.

Stephano: Monster, help to bear this away where my hogshead of wine is or I'll turn you out of my kingdom. Go to, carry this.

Trinculo: And this.

Stephano: Ay, and this.

(Enter spirits in shape of dogs. They bark and chase Caliban, Stephano, and Trinculo off stage.)

Ariel: Hark, they roar!

Prospero: Let them be hunted soundly. At this hour lie at my mercy all mine enemies. Shortly shall all my work be ended, and you, Ariel, shall have the freedom of the air. But for a little while still follow me and do me service. Now does my project gather to a head. My charms crack not. My spirits obey. How's the day?

Ariel: On the sixth hour, at which time, my lord, you said our work should cease.

Prospero: I did say so when first I raised the tempest. Say my spirit, how fares the king and his followers?

Ariel: Confined together, just as you left them. All prisoners, sir, they cannot budge till your release. The king, his brother, and yours, are all three distracted and the remainder mourning over them, but chiefly him that you called "The good old lord Gonzalo," his tears run down his beard. If you now beheld them, your affections would become tender.

Prospero: Dost thou think so, spirit?

Ariel: Mine would, sir, were I human.

Prospero: And mine shall. Go release them, Ariel. My charms I'll break, their senses I'll restore, and they shall be themselves.

Ariel: I'll fetch them, sir.

(Ariel exits.)

Prospero: I have bedimmed the noontide sun, called forth the mutinous winds. To the dread rattling thunder have I given fire, the strong-based promontory have I made shake, and by the roots plucked up the pine and cedar. But this rough magic I here abjure. I'll break my staff, bury it certain fathoms in the earth, and deeper than ever plummet sound I'll drown my book. (Enter Ariel, followed by Alonzo, Gonzalo, Sebastian, Antonio, and Adrian, all in astonishment. They enter Prospero's magic circle and stand spellbound.) There stand for you are spell stopped. Holy Gonzalo, honourable man, mine eyes fall drops. O good Gonzalo, my true preserver, I will pay thy graces home both in word and deed. Most cruelly didst thou, Alonzo, use me and my daughter. Thy brother was also in the act. I do forgive thee, unnatural though thou art. Not one of them that looks on me would know me. Ariel, fetch me my clothes as I used to be, the Duke of Milan. Quickly spirit, for soon thou shalt be free.

Ariel: (Helps dress Prospero while singing)
Where the bee lights, there light I.
In a cowslip's bell I lie.
There I couch when owls do cry.
On the bat's back I do fly after summer merrily.
Merrily, merrily shall I live now,
Under the blossom that hangs on the bough.

Prospero: Why, that's my dainty Ariel. I shall miss thee, but yet thou shalt have freedom. So, to the king's ship, invisible as thou art. There shalt thou find the mariners asleep under the hatches. The Master and the Boatswain being awake, enforce them to this place.

Ariel: I drink the air before me and return before your pulse twice beat.

(Ariel exits.)

Gonzalo: All torment, trouble, wonder, and amazement inhabits here. Some heavenly power guide us out of this fearful country.

Prospero: Behold, sir king, the wronged Duke of Milan, Prospero. For more assurance, I bid thee a hearty welcome.

Alonzo: Whether thou beest he or a spirit, I know not. Thy pulse beats as of flesh and blood. Thy dukedom I resign and do entreat thou pardon me my wrongs. But how should Prospero be living and be here?

Prospero: First, noble friend, let me embrace thine age whose honour cannot be measured.

Gonzalo: Whether this be or be not, I do not know.

Prospero: Welcome, my friends, all. (To Sebastian and Antonio.) But you, my brace of lords, were I so minded, I here could justify you as traitors. At this time I will tell no tales.

Sebastian: (Aside.)
The devil speaks in him.

Prospero: For you, most wicked sir, whom to call brother would even infect my mouth, I do forgive the rankest fault, all of them, and require my dukedom of thee, which I know thou must restore.

Alonzo: If thou beest Prospero, give us particulars of thy preservation, how thou hast met us here upon this shore where I have lost my dear son Ferdinand.

Prospero: A great loss to me, for I have lost my daughter.

Alonzo: A daughter? When did you lose your daughter?

Prospero: In this last tempest. Know for certain that I am Prospero and lord of this island.

(Draws curtain to reveal Miranda and Ferdinand inside tent.)

Alonzo: If this prove a vision of the island, one dear son shall I twice lose.

Sebastian: Antonio most high miracle.

(Ferdinand kneels before his father, Alonzo.)

Alonzo: Arise, and say how thou camest here.

Miranda: O wonder! O brave new world that has such wonderful people in it!

Prospero: 'Tis new to thee.

Alonzo: Who is this maid? Is she the goddess that brought us together again?

Ferdinand: Sir, she is mortal. I chose her when I could not ask you for advice. She is the daughter of this famous Duke of Milan from whom I have received a second life.

Gonzalo: Look down, you gods, and on this couple drop a blessed crown.

Alonzo: I say, Amen, Gonzalo. (To Ferdinand and Miranda.) Give me your hands. We wish you joy.

(Re-enter Ariel with Master and Boatswain.)

Gonzalo: O look, sir, look, sir, here is more of us. I prophesied if a gallows were on land, this fellow could not drown.

Boatswain: The best news is that we found our king and company. The next, our ship is ready for sea.

Ariel: (Aside.)
Sir, all this service have I done.

Prospero: (Aside.)
My tricky spirit.

Ariel: (Aside.)
Was it well done?

Prospero: (Aside.)
Bravely! Thou shalt be free.

Alonzo: This is a strange a maze as ever men trod.

Prospero: Sir, do not infest your mind with the strangeness of this business. I'll explain it all to you shortly. (To Ariel.) Come hither, spirit. Set Caliban and his companions free. Untie the spell. (Exit Ariel.) There are yet missing of your company some few odd lads that you remember not.

(Re-enter Ariel driving in Caliban, Stephano, and Trinculo.)

Stephano: Every man for himself. Courage, bully monster, courage!

Caliban: I'm afraid my master will chastise me.

Sebastian: Ha-ha! What things are these, my lord Antonio? Will money buy them?

Antonio: Very likely.

Prospero: Mark these men, my lords. This mis-shapen knave, his mother was a wicked woman and one so strong that could control the moon. These three have robbed me and this evil one had plotted with them to take my life. Two of these fellows you must know and own. This thing of darkness I acknowledge mine.

Caliban: I shall be pinched to death.

Alonzo: Is this not Stephano, my butler? Is this not Trinculo? (Pointing at Caliban.)
This is a strange thing that I look on.

Prospero: (To Caliban.)
Go to my cell. Take with you your companions. If you wish pardon, move quickly.

Caliban: Ay, that I will, and I'll be wise hereafter. What a thrice double fool was I to take this man for a god and worship him.

Prospero: Go! (Exit Caliban, Stephano, and Trinculo. To Alonzo.)

Sir, I invite your highness and your train to my poor cell, where you shall take your rest for this one night. In the morn I'll bring you to your ship and so to Naples, where I hope to see the nuptial of these our dearly beloved.

Alonzo: I long to hear the story of your life which must take strangely to the ear.

Prospero: I'll deliver all, and promise you calm seas, auspicious gales, and sail so expeditious that shall catch your royal fleet far off. (Aside to Ariel.) My Ariel, chick, that is thy charge. Then to the elements be free, and fare thou well.

Ariel: Farewell, master!

(All exit except Prospero.)

Prospero: Our revels now are ended. These our actors, as I foretold you, were all spirits, and are melted into air, into thin air. And, like the baseless fabric of this vision, the cloud-capped towers, the gorgeous palaces, the solemn temples, the globe itself, yea, all which it inherit, shall dissolve and, like this substantial pageant fade, leave not a track behind. We are such stuff as dreams are made on, and our little life is rounded with a sleep.